I0436272

Editor-in-Chief and Founder:
  Lyndon H. LaRouche, Jr.
Editorial Board: *Lyndon H. LaRouche, Jr. , Helga
  Zepp-LaRouche, Robert Ingraham, Tony
  Papert, Gerald Rose, Dennis Small, Jeffrey
  Steinberg, William Wertz*
Co-Editors: *Robert Ingraham, Tony Papert*
Managing Editor: *Nancy Spannaus*
Technology: *Marsha Freeman*
Books: *Katherine Notley*
Ebooks: *Richard Burden*
Graphics: *Alan Yue*
Photos: *Stuart Lewis*
Circulation Manager: *Stanley Ezrol*

INTELLIGENCE DIRECTORS
Counterintelligence: *Jeffrey Steinberg, Michele
  Steinberg*
Economics: *John Hoefle, Marcia Merry Baker,
  Paul Gallagher*
History: *Anton Chaitkin*
Ibero-America: *Dennis Small*
Russia and Eastern Europe: *Rachel Douglas*
United States: *Debra Freeman*

INTERNATIONAL BUREAUS
Bogotá: *Miriam Redondo*
Berlin: *Rainer Apel*
Copenhagen: *Tom Gillesberg*
Houston: *Harley Schlanger*
Lima: *Sara Madueño*
Melbourne: *Robert Barwick*
Mexico City: *Gerardo Castilleja Chávez*
New Delhi: *Ramtanu Maitra*
Paris: *Christine Bierre*
Stockholm: *Ulf Sandmark*
United Nations, N.Y.C.: *Leni Rubinstein*
Washington, D.C.: *William Jones*
Wiesbaden: *Göran Haglund*

ON THE WEB
e-mail: eirns@larouchepub.com
www.larouchepub.com
www.executiveintelligencereview.com
www.larouchepub.com/eiw
Webmaster: *John Sigerson*
Assistant Webmaster: *George Hollis*
Editor, Arabic-language edition: *Hussein Askary*

EIR (ISSN 0273-6314) *is published weekly
(50 issues), by EIR News Service, Inc.,
P.O. Box 17390, Washington, D.C. 20041-0390.
(703) 777-9451*

European Headquarters: E.I.R. GmbH, Postfach
Bahnstrasse 9a, D-65205, Wiesbaden, Germany
Tel: 49-611-73650
Homepage: http://www.eirna.com
e-mail: eirna@eirna.com
Director: Georg Neudecker

Montreal, Canada: 514-461-1557

Denmark: EIR - Danmark, Sankt Knuds Vej 11,
basement left, DK-1903 Frederiksberg, Denmark.
Tel.: +45 35 43 60 40, Fax: +45 35 43 87 57. e-mail:
eirdk@hotmail.com.

Mexico City: EIR, Sor Juana Inés de la Cruz 242-2
Col. Agricultura C.P. 11360
Delegación M. Hidalgo, México D.F.
Tel. (5525) 5318-2301
eirmexico@gmail.com

Canada Post Publication Sales Agreement
#40683579

Postmaster: Send all address changes to *EIR*, P.O.
Box 17390, Washington, D.C. 20041-0390.

Signed articles in *EIR* represent the views of the
authors, and not necessarily those of the Editorial
Board.

Crushing of O'Malley Marks Drive for War

Crushing of O'Malley Marks Drive for War

Feb. 2—On Thursday, Feb. 4, Lyndon LaRouche will be holding an emergency dialogue with LPAC activists on the implications of the brutal termination of the presidential campaign of Martin O'Malley, and what this signals about the immediate danger of general war.

In the days immediately preceding the Iowa caucus, LaRouche had made a pointed intervention to set out the policy preconditions for his support for an O'Malley presidency, with the idea that this act on his part would force some of the leading enemies of the American Republic to play their hand, and reveal their intentions.

LaRouche's conclusion, following the abrupt termination of the O'Malley presidential campaign, even before the final Iowa results were announced, was that leading British circles, controlling the Barack Obama Presidency, are desperately escalating their preparations for war against Russia and China. The actions against O'Malley were, in effect, a red dye indication of the war preparations already well-underway. The fact that there were escalating British Crown provocations against Russian President Vladimir Putin, coincident with the actions against O'Malley, sealed the case.

The timing of these events was driven by the fact that the entire trans-Atlantic financial system—the British System—was in an accelerating crash process, as indicated by the meltdown of the entire Italian banking system, at a more rapid rate than the earlier collapses of Greece, Portugal, and Ireland.

These British Empire forces, including their Obama Presidency, are committed to the rapid depopulation of the planet, through warfare and other means. The coincidence of the breakdown crisis, the over-reaction to the LaRouche intervention on behalf of a viable O'Malley candidacy, and the dramatic escalation in targeted provocations against both Russia and China—coming from London and the White House—is the clearest evidence available that mankind is moving into a moment of grave crisis.

The fact that top leaders in both Russia and China are aware, to a great extent, of the significance of these developments, means that there are counter-measures that can be taken, if the full implications of the recent days' events are understood.

On Thursday night, Feb. 4, at 9 p.m., Lyndon La-Rouche will hold his weekly Fireside Chat (details can be obtained from local LPAC organizations) to discuss these extraordinary developments. On Saturday, Feb. 6, LaRouche will hold his weekly Manhattan dialogue, with a live audience, on the same emergency situation and what must be done.

These two dialogues are must-attend events for all citizens serious about preventing a near-term plunge into a global war that will rapidly escalate into a thermonuclear confrontation, jeopardizing the very survival of humankind. Be prepared for an intense and frank discussion and for an extraordinary mobilization.

EIR Contents

www.larouchepub.com Volume 43, Number 6, February 5, 2016

**Cover
This Week**

*Hydrogen bomb
test on Bikini
Atoll in the
Pacific in 1954.*

I. Throw the Bums Out!

Our Electoral Campaign Policy

Jan. 28—"We want active support, from us, to boost O'Malley's campaign, because it's necessary that his campaign be boosted," Lyndon LaRouche said to associates Jan. 27. Take the things we recognize in O'Malley's policy, as opposed to maybe some side issues, which are not the same thing.

We're going to boost this intervention, with La-Rouche's name on it,— especially from and through Manhattan and nearby points. That's our strongest point. LaRouche's Saturday dialogues with the Manhattan Project will be our leading voice on this issue.

And what we're saying to O'Malley is: We're suggesting strongly that you focus yourself on your *own* policy directly. We support your making this the issue, and we recognize our responsibility to make a contribution to that effect. We recommend O'Malley follow the indicated policy, and we'll commit ourselves to support that policy; we make ourselves answerable to support that program in the election. "I'll personally support his option if he wants to follow that option," LaRouche said.

We're moving in to unscramble some of the things that are going on in the election campaign right now. If we step in with my name on this thing, LaRouche said, that is going to cause an effect. And I personally will be supporting his option if he wants to follow that option. The message is that it's time for clarity on campaign policy. We have to have our own national campaign policy, which we thrust into the election process. And we say, "Do you want to do something with us? This is what we're doing!" If we do that now, we get in there, and we change the character of the thing. What's wrong with Bernie Sanders, and what's wrong with Hillary? The problem is that these guys are fakers.

Neither he nor she has any clear policy. The United States requires a human option as op-posed to Hillary and Bernie Sanders. O'Malley has the option, if he wants to narrow the issues, of presenting something which will outflank these guys.

I strongly recommend that the O'Malley campaign team do this: Get rid of the dubious things, and go for a straightforward address to what the problem is, because Hillary is a fraud,— her record is that of a fraud, since she capitulated to Obama. She's totally a stooge for Obama. A vote for Hillary is a vote for Obama, and we're not voting for Obama. Sanders is the same kind

LaRouche declared on Jan. 27: O'Malley is not certain that he has the authority to be the leading candidate, but he must step forward now. Here, the relevant screen shot from the LaRouche PAC website.

of thing: He's an opportunist who tries to patch something together to fool people.

We don't see any clear option coming from him or her. You don't want a "line,"— you want to solve the problems of the United States.

Tactical Surprise

It's not about what O'Malley's candidacy is; the point is that his candidacy is the only thing that's fit to be supported. Now, if he's willing to do that program, what we can do is flank this operation. You come in with a fresh approach, and say that Hillary's actually a stooge for Obama. You say that in fact of practice, she's a stooge for Obama. And she gets closer all the time, every time she makes a move. And Sanders doesn't do anything really.... He tries to make a line, spill a line out. Somebody attacks his line, he adjusts his line. You don't want a line, you want to solve the problems of the United States.

We have to do a pre-emptive thing; just do something that is completely different from what these guys are trying to adapt to. And present the case. Simply say that O'Malley has raised certain questions, and these questions have to be clarified. Because we don't see any option for the coming election. We don't see any sane option except that, so far. He's the only significant candidate, who so far has represented anything that fits the purpose of the United States. So, he's the best we've got; we'll go with the best we've got.

His weakness is the fact that he thinks that he is not a leading candidate; therefore he has a modesty approach in the way he reacts, and says, "Well, I'm not yet in the position where I can make the big fist. I'm a good candidate; I'm probably the best candidate that we have available, but I don't yet have the position of a leading candidate." Nothing complicated; it's that simple.

We operate on the basis of the element of surprise: of creating a tactical surprise. We go out and say we like *this* bum, rather than that bum. It's a fresh approach,— also a refreshing approach.

O'Malley is not certain that he has the authority to shoot out to be the leading candidate for the election. But the issue is not whether you think you have the authority to do this: the issue is whether you understand that it must be done. Because Hillary is a disaster, and Bernie Sanders is a different kind of disaster.

This is not one of these gimmicks; this is simple truth.

"Hey, guys: off the bullshit," is what you should be aiming for.

What changes people is when they realize that they've been idiots; that they've been suckers. Because they've been told they have to do this, they have to do that, they have to be practical. Well, let's get rid of that "practical" stuff. Go to the issue. Go to the effect; go straight to the effect.

Why don't we just tell people that what they've been given as a choice of candidacies to support is a damn fraud; a farce. Get rid of the farce. What do you mean, get rid of the farce? Well, you've got Hillary; she's a fraud; and you've got Sanders, and we're not sure what his species is.

It should be fun, because if it's done clearly, it should be "Wake up people! Are you so dumb? Do you want Hillary? Do you trust Bernie Sanders?"

You've got two candidates you're really talking about in the Democratic Party. You've got Hillary; she's an Obama stooge. She'll continue to be an Obama stooge. And Sanders? Vermont is ashamed of this guy. Dump him! Dump her! And what have you got?

O'Malley has had limited leadership for the campaign period, now. All you have to do is to get him to step forward now. Why now? Because these two jokers are not worth anything! "Hey, citizen!"

The crucial issue is to get clear what we mean: indicating why O'Malley is hesitating to take a heavy role in the election campaign. Because he doesn't think he has the muscle presented to him to do it. On the question of positive things, he'll function. But on the question of being charged with the leading responsibility, that is something that makes him a little bit nervous, because he's not sure he's in a position to do that yet. That's why my intervention, if it's done properly, will have an effect, LaRouche said. Because there are a lot of people who know me, know my name and what I've done,— know my history. You put that in there, and no one can really forecast what the result might be. But anything we would have as a result, would be far better than anything we would have by not doing it.

And so, you try to stir the thing up. Put more features in it. Because Hillary is a fraudster, and Sanders is not exactly a gentleman.

The way the political operation is headed now, everything is being set up to try to get it under control. And if you go into that with an approach which is not on that agenda of planning and control, then you can tip the whole thing into collapse.

Now let's make our intention clear, not as a rumor, but as an explicit intention.

Who Is Martin O'Malley?

by Matthew Ogden

Jan. 29—*Matthew Ogden opened up LaRouche PAC's regular weekly webcast of Friday, Jan. 29, with a report on Democratic Presidential pre-candidate Martin O'Malley, as edited and excerpted below.*

Mr. LaRouche has taken the initiative over the past 48 hours to go on the record and urge Martin O'Malley, one of the three official candidates for the Democratic Party's nominee for President, to become emboldened in his Presidential campaign, as a serious contender for the Presidency, by returning to the core theme of reinstating Glass-Steagall, a policy which remains the defining issue of this campaign, and a policy which O'Malley asserted as his top priority from the very beginning of his campaign, which earned him the moniker "Wall Street's Enemy No. 1" right off the bat. As Fox Business News reporter Charles Gasparino said in June of last year, "Martin O'Malley is now *persona non grata*, Public Enemy No. 1, in the halls of Goldman Sachs; in the halls of BlackRock, the big money-management firm; all throughout Wall Street right now. O'Malley is the last person Wall Street would want to win."

This week, LaRouche urged O'Malley to embrace that identity as "Wall Street's Public Enemy No. 1," and to become much more aggressive and bold as a candidate on those terms. Mr. LaRouche stated, "It is obvious to me that O'Malley's views have a certain degree of convergence with my own views on this subject, on the necessity to shut down Wall Street before we are destroyed as a nation by it."

So, for the sake of the American people, you who

NBC News/Standard YouTube license

Martin O'Malley confronts Hillary Clinton in the Democratic candidates' debate in South Carolina, Jan. 17, 2016.

are viewing this webcast, and even perhaps for the sake of certain people within O'Malley's campaign, we thought it important to begin our broadcast tonight by reviewing a bit of what Gov. O'Malley's position has been on this question, especially on the critical issue of restoring Glass-Steagall, which was what originally earned him the ire of Wall Street and its fellow travellers.

Called for Glass-Steagall Before Announcing

Prior to even announcing his campaign for the Presidency, Martin O'Malley telegraphed what the main focus of his candidacy would be, by writing a very prominent op-ed in the March 19 issue of the *Des Moines Register*, the newspaper of record in the state of Iowa. The op-ed was titled, "Prevent Another Crash. Reform Wall Street." He began as follows:

Seven years after the Wall Street meltdown, Americans are still experiencing the fall-out. Although job creation rates and GDP—along with bank bonuses and corporate profits—are on the upswing, these statistics mask the lingering hardship of millions of families that traces itself back to Wall Street's reckless behavior.... We were forced to save our economy, by bailing out big banks. Now, we have a responsibility to correct the mistakes of our more recent past to prevent another crash. To do that, we must acknowledge that ... the 2010 Dodd-Frank Act did not go nearly far enough.

The most serious structural reform we can make is reinstating the 1933 Glass-Steagall Act that kept commercial banks separate from investment banks. Under Glass-Steagall, our country did not see a major financial crisis for nearly 70 years. If that law hadn't been repealed, in 1999, the crash would have been contained. The largest banks on Wall Street should be broken up into more manageable institutions. Today, five banks control half of the financial industry's $15 trillion in assets....

Unfortunately, while many good people who work in finance and in Congress understand our vulnerability to another crash, further reform faces an uphill climb against very powerful special interests.... It's time to put the national interest before the interests of Wall Street. The future of our economy ... depends on it.

swiss-image.ch/Remy Steinegger

Fox Business News reporter in June 2015: "Martin O'Malley is now persona non grata, Public Enemy No. 1, in the halls of Goldman Sachs [and] all throughout Wall Street right now. Here, Lloyd Blankfein, chairman and CEO of Goldman Sachs Group.

So that was the op-ed that Martin O'Malley wrote in the *Des Moines Register* before he even announced his campaign.

On May 30, 2015, O'Malley made his official announcement as a candidate for the Presidency at a site overlooking Fort McHenry in Baltimore. He related the story of how, in the War of 1812, the British had just invaded Washington and had burnt down the White House and the other Federal buildings, and he said that the people of Maryland could see the glow of the fires in Washington, all the way from Baltimore. He said, "We knew that they were coming for us. But, instead of digging graves," he said, "we dug trenches, and we fought to save the American Republic that hung by a very slender thread. And that fighting spirit," he said, "at that time, is what's needed now, especially as we face, today, the impoverishment and the destruction of our nation's people, by a handful of very wealthy, nominally, Wall Street banks, which have literally taken our government over, taken our government hostage, and used it to turn our economic system upside down and against the very people whom it's supposed to serve."

What he said in his prepared remarks, was as follows:

Our economic and political system is upside down and backwards; and it is time to turn it around. What happened to our economy—what happened to the American Dream—did not happen by chance. Nor was it merely the result of global forces somehow beyond our control. Powerful, wealthy special interests here at home have used our government to create—in our own country—an economy that is leaving a majority of our people behind. An economy that has so concentrated wealth in the hands of the very few, that it has taken opportunity from the homes of the many. An economy where a majority of our people are unheard, unseen, un-needed, and left to conclude that their lives and their labors are literally worth less today than they were yesterday, ... and will be worth less still tomorrow. ... We are allowing our land of opportunity to be turned into a land of inequality. Main Street struggles, while Wall Street soars. ... Our economy isn't money, our economy is people—all of our people. We measure success by the growing prosperity and security of our people—all of our people. ... We must put our national interest first. ... But we cannot rebuild the American Dream here at home by catering to the voices of the privileged and the powerful. Let's be honest. They were the ones who turned our economy upside-down in the first place. And they are the only ones who are benefitting from it. ... [Therefore] we need to restore Glass-Steagall, and if a bank is too big to fail without wrecking our nation's economy ... then it needs to be broken up before it breaks us ... again.

That was his campaign announcement. Obviously a central issue.

Too Big to Fail—or Jail

Then, in July 2015, O'Malley issued a campaign White Paper, highlighting his policy of reinstating Glass-Steagall, in which he warned, explicitly, of the danger of another devastating meltdown of the Wall Street financial system, were Glass-Steagall not to be reinstated immediately. This ten-page White Paper from O'Malley's campaign, is titled, "Protecting the American Dream from Another Wall Street Crash." Very briefly, what it included was the following:

Governor O'Malley knows that the American Dream today remains out of reach for too many families. To attack this problem, it will take a multi-pronged and fearlessly progressive approach to addressing economic inequality. But the results of any steps we take as a nation to raise wages, ensure retirement security, and make the dream of home ownership a reality can be wiped out in an instant in another Wall Street crash. We need to protect America's economy. And we can only do it by implementing strong accountability and structural reforms that build upon the Dodd-Frank Act and put an end to too-big-to-fail, too-big-to-manage, and too-big-to-jail financial firms.

Under the heading, "Breaking up the too-big-to-fail, too-big-to-manage, too-big-to-jail Firms Before They Break Us," O'Malley says, "...[A] handful of too-big-to-fail ... megabanks continue to pose an enormous risk: to our financial system, the economy, and American families. As President, O'Malley will work tirelessly to eliminate the unique danger posed by too-big-to-fail banks, by making the following structural reforms: Break up the biggest banks and separate risky investment banking from ordinary commercial banking."

And then he says, "For 70 years, the 1933 Glass-Steagall Act kept the U.S. economy safe from major financial crises by requiring commercial banks to be separate from investment banks, to prevent them from putting everyday Americans' deposits at risk. If Glass-Steagall hadn't been repealed in 1999, the financial crisis would likely have been far less severe."

So, as President,

Martin O'Malley will immediately reinstate Glass-Steagall. The Volcker Rule, sometimes referred to as "Glass-Steagall Lite," is excessively complex; providing too many opportunities for banks to exploit loopholes and ambiguities. O'Malley will introduce legislation to once again separate traditional banks from riskier financial services, while updating protections to account for new banking activities and prevent the new rules from being watered down. This will be one of his top priorities.

In conjunction with this White Paper, O'Malley issued an Open Letter on July 9 to the Wall Street megabanks, in which he reiterated his commitment to reinstating Glass-Steagall, and then, went through measures to send bank executives to jail, to identify their criminal complicity, not to let them off the hook—major prosecution. What he said in this Open Letter, which was circulated very widely at the time and drew a lot of attention, was:

> As you've heard, I've expressed grave concern about the state of our national economy, especially as it relates to the behavior of a select group of financial institutions on Wall Street—the institutions that you work for and represent. I have called for significant structural and accountability reforms—like reinstating Glass-Steagall and increasing enforcement at the SEC, DOJ, and other agencies and departments—to prevent another economic crash and protect hard-working families from losing their jobs, homes, and life savings once again.

And then he goes on to describe what has happened since 2008 because Glass-Steagall was not reinstated at that time. He says, "The high-risk, reckless, and illegal activities of your megabanks were the primary cause of the 2008 crash, which caused the worst recession since the Great Depression, cost the American economy an estimated $14-22 trillion. Today, your—too-big-to-fail, too-big-to-manage, too-big-to-jail—megabanks pose an enormous risk to the financial system, the economy, and American families. They are so big and so interconnected with the entire financial system, that the failure of one or more of them could cause the collapse of the entire U.S. economy."

He continues, "After several misguided regulatory measures taken in the 1990's," including the repeal of Glass-Steagall, "your handful of megabanks went from having assets of approximately 15% of our country's GDP, to now having assets of nearly 65% of our GDP. As your megabanks grew in size, who gained from it? Credit card fees didn't get smaller. Mortgage rates didn't go down. The median wages of Americans certainly didn't increase. The only tangible gain we've seen from your institutions' explosion in size is your ability to concentrate unprecedented power and wealth in the hands of your executives and to acquire the guarantee that all of your risky bets will be covered by taxpayers. ... So here's the bad news—for you: As President, I have no plans to let up on you. I'll work tirelessly to eliminate the unique danger posed by the handful of too-big-to-fail banks," including through the reinstatement of Glass-Steagall.

And, finally, as those of you who have watched the series of Democratic Party debates well know, Martin O'Malley has consistently injected Glass-Steagall into the discussion, as a top priority, and called Hillary Clinton out on her lies in that regard, and has discussed this as a top priority for *preventing* another devastating crash of the financial system, and protecting the lives and the livelihoods of the American people in the event that such a crash occurs. What Mr. LaRouche had to say about this earlier today, is that this is not a matter of "if"; this is not a matter of "when." That crash is happening *now*.

So, as I said, Mr. LaRouche has made very clear public statements in the last 48 hours, including in his discussion with activists across the United States in his weekly Fireside Chat last night, urging Martin O'Malley to embrace his identity as Wall Street's Enemy No. 1, by concentrating on this core issue—the reinstatement of Glass-Steagall, the shutting down of these Wall Street banks, and the revival of a very clear Franklin Roosevelt First 100 Days New Deal policy to save the United States.

Hillary: The Obama Stooge Bernie: The Bullshitter

by Gerry Rose

Feb. 1—Ever since Wall Street declared Democratic Party presidential candidate Martin O'Malley to be "Public Enemy No. 1," the mainstream media has worked overtime to sell the illusion that the real race for the Democratic Party's nomination is a two-way race between Hillary Clinton and Bernie Sanders.

The reality is that the Wall Street speculators who have destroyed the nation's productive economy and driven tens of millions of American citizens into despair and drug addiction over the fifteen-year span of the Bush and Obama Presidencies, are engaged in an all-out effort to control the Presidential race and hoodwink the American people. To say that Wall Street is "comfortable" with Hillary Clinton would

be a dramatic understatement. Her repeated attacks on the proposal to re-enact Franklin Roosevelt's Glass-Steagall legislation and her vocal backing for the fraudulent Dodd-Frank legislation, have made her a darling of the Wall Street crowd, as evidenced by the $6 million donation given to Priorities USA Action, a leading "super PAC" for the Clinton campaign, by mega-speculator and drug pusher George Soros.

Meanwhile, despite the fact that many leftists and "millenials" have been dazzled by the rhetoric of Bernie Sanders—in the same way that their parents and older brothers and sisters were conned by the media hype surrounding Barack Obama in 2008—Sanders is under-

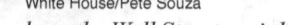
White House/Pete Souza
creative commons/Gage Skidmore

Hillary Clinton: Obama owns her. Bernie Sanders: the Wall Street socialist.

stood by Wall Street to be a non-serious buffoon, who poses no danger to their interests and has no chance of ever being elected. He is there merely to create the illusion of a tightly controlled two-way race. At the end of the day, Sanders is fodder for some of the better Saturday Night Live skits of this election season—and not a serious presidential candidate.

Hillary

Hillary Clinton's biggest problem is that she was broken by President Obama and his inner circle of Valerie Jarrett, Susan Rice, Samantha Power, and Michelle Obama. As Obama's Secretary of State, Hillary Clinton was forced to do Obama's bidding, even when she knew it was wrong and would jeopardize her own political future. By serving in the Obama Administration for four brutal years, she became an accessory to most of the Obama crimes, and ultimately became responsible for Obama's "bodyguard of lies," to borrow the phrase of historian Anthony Cave-Brown.

Hillary Clinton was not always an Obama tool. During the first two years of the Obama presidency, Clinton, as Secretary of State, worked closely with then National Security Adviser Gen. James Jones and then Defense Secretary Robert Gates, to create a counter-pole to the Obama inner circle at the White House and the National Security Council.

That containment alliance ultimately fell apart. First, Gen. Jones resigned as National Security Adviser, having discovered that his deputy, Thomas Donilon, was working to undermine his efforts. Robert Gates was adamant that he would have nothing to do with Donilon, whom he described as a vicious "political hatchet-man" with no background in national security.

In early 2011, Defense Secretary Gates and Clinton had a falling out over Libya. President Obama and his

The premeditated burning of the U.S. Mission in Benghazi, Libya on Sept. 11, 2012.

inner circle of responsibility-to-protect (R2P) "humanitarian" interventionists, decided—along with the British and French—to oust Libyan leader Muammar Qadaffi. Gates adamantly opposed the scheme, warning that the proposed no-fly zone to protect "innocent" Benghazi citizens from government reprisals, would mean that the United States and its allies were committed to all-out regime change. Both Russia and China had been lied to by Obama's UN Ambassador Susan Rice, and were persuaded to abstain during the crucial UN Security Council vote on the authorization to use military force to protect the civilian population of eastern Libya. The goal, as Gates knew, was regime change. Rather than participate in such a colossal blunder, Gates resigned.[1]

Hillary, in contrast, went over to the dark side in the Qadaffi affair. She embraced her sworn enemies, led by Susan Rice and Samantha Power, and wholeheartedly backed the ouster of the Libyan leader. By no later than that capitulation, Hillary was owned by the Obama camp, despite all the personal animosities and resentments. For Hillary, this was a moral *punctum saliens.* When you cross that line psychologically, it is very hard

---

1. Gates had come into the George W. Bush Administration in the aftermath of the 2003 Iraq invasion and regime change swindle, and had witnessed the destabilization of the entire region, beginning at that time.

to turn back, especially when you are driven by political ambition.

After months of U.S., British, and French air and ground operations, Qadaffi was overthrown and was physically cornered. The choice fell to President Obama, British Prime Minister David Cameron, and French President Nicolas Sarkozy, whether to have Qadaffi assassinated or captured. They decided that Qadaffi was too dangerous alive and ordered him murdered in cold blood.

Hillary Clinton was all-in. In a gale of giddy laughter, she invoked the words of Julius Caesar in summarizing the U.S. role in the murder of Qadaffi in her widely-publicized quip: "We came, we saw, he died."

The Qadaffi assassination was the prelude to Hillary Clinton's darkest moment of capitulation to the Obama monster. On Sept. 11, 2012, less than a year after the Qadaffi "executive action," U.S. Ambassador to Libya Christopher Stevens was murdered, along with three other American officials, at the U.S. mission in Benghazi and a CIA annex a mile away. The premeditated attack, on the anniversary of the original 9/11 attacks, was carried out by an al-Qaeda affiliate, Ansar al-Sharia.

According to author Edward Klein, whose book *Blood Feud* recounts the Obama-Clinton family wars, Hillary Clinton was receiving hourly reports from the U.S. Deputy Chief of Mission in Libya, Gregory Hicks, who was in Tripoli running the embassy on the day of the attacks. Hicks conveyed reports received from the scene in Benghazi directly to Clinton, as well as to the White House Situation Room. For Hicks and for the people on the ground in Benghazi, there was no doubt that al-Qaeda had carried out a heavily armed terrorist attack. There never was a demonstration outside the U.S. mission, supposedly protesting a virtually unknown video slandering the Prophet Mohammed. It simply didn't happen.

Klein recounts what happened next, drawing upon interviews with eyewitnesses, including close Clinton aides:

> By 10 p.m. on Sept. 11, 2012, when Hillary Clinton received a call from President Obama, she was one of the most thoroughly briefed officials in Washington on the unfolding disaster in Benghazi, Libya.

She knew that Ambassador Christopher Stevens and a communications operator were dead, and that the attackers had launched a well-coordinated mortar assault on the CIA annex, which would cost the lives of two more Americans.

She had no doubt that a terrorist attack had been launched against America on the anniversary of 9/11. However, when Hillary picked up the phone and heard Obama's voice, she learned the president had other ideas in mind. With less than two months before Election Day, he was still boasting that he had al-Qaeda on the run.

If the truth about Benghazi became known, it would blow that argument out of the water.

"Hillary was stunned when she heard the president talk about the Benghazi attack," one of her top legal advisers said in an interview. "Obama wanted her to say that the attack had been a spontaneous demonstration triggered by an obscure video on the Internet that demeaned the Prophet Mohammed."

According to Klein's account, Clinton conferred with her husband, former President Bill Clinton, and they concluded that if Hillary balked at Obama's order, she would have to resign, and would likely be held to blame for an Obama re-election defeat. Hillary Clinton, at that moment, completed her ultimate capitulation to Barack Obama. She put out the press release that Obama demanded of her, linking the attack to "spontaneous protests" over the scurrilous video.

Hillary Clinton's presidential ambitions so clouded her judgment that she became complicit in a crime that remains the subject of intense Congressional scrutiny. Whether the full truth about Benghazi ever comes out or not, it was yet another breaking point for Hillary Clinton. Her capitulation to Obama was complete. He owned her.

Bernie

Contrary to the mainstream media myth, it was not Bernie Sanders who put the issue of Wall Street and the urgent need for Glass-Steagall and a new Pecora Commission on the table for the 2016 presidential elections. It was Gov. Martin O'Malley. Sanders' johnny-come-lately endorsement of Glass-Steagall was designed to do one thing and one thing only—to take attention away from the serious attacks on Wall Street emanating from O'Malley.

Sanders has a media "rep," stemming from his long-time claim of being a socialist, of being some sort of a leftist "progressive." The reality is, as born out in the *Congressional Record,* that since being elected to the U.S. Senate, Sanders has voted 98% of the time with the Senate Democratic leadership.

Sanders is no Jeremy Corbyn. Corbyn, the British Labour Party leader, is not only hated by the establishment for his support of Glass-Steagall; he has also refused to support any sanctions against Russia and China, and wants to take down Great Britain's entire nuclear weapons program. He has also—and most importantly—refused to bow before the Queen. By contrast, Sanders has voted for every single sanctions bill against Putin, against whom he has a stated visceral hatred. Sanders also hates Iran and has repeatedly voted for sanctions against that nation. Sanders has supported every authorization of military force (AUMF) and every trade-war measure against China. Not quite a "peacenik."

One progressive has this to say about Sanders:

Even so, while Bernie may come across as sincere about class politics, make no mistake, he is a militarist that isn't about to challenge U.S. supremacy. He supported the ugly war on Kosovo, the invasion of Afghanistan, funding for the endless Iraq disaster as well as the losing and misguided War on Terror. He voted in favor of Clinton's 1996 Anti-Terrorism and Effective Death Penalty Act, which expanded the federal death penalty and acted as the precursor to the PATRIOT Act.[2]

U.S. Air Force/Tech Sgt. Joseph Swafford

Bernie supported the war on Kosovo, the invasion of Afghanistan, and funding for the endless Iraq disaster and the so-called War on Terror. Here, U.S. soldiers enter a U.S. Army CH-47 Chinook helicopter at an Afghan combat outpost.

In fact, Sanders comes out of a wing of the American "left," that went from Socialist to Social Democrat to neoconservative in foreign policy, defense, and national security.

It was with good reason that these types, during the 1950s and 1960s, were known as "State Department socialists." Because of their zeal to dodge the bullets of McCarthyism, they became hardcore advocates of the Cold War.

Sanders is a complete fraud, an empty shell, without any moral convictions. The only issue for which his sincerity can not be doubted is that he is the most radically green candidate on either slate. He proposes ten million green jobs, which would wipe out what is left of actual science and industry in the United States and destroy what is left of the productive labor force.

Most "insiders" believe that the promotion of Bernie and the "mainstream media" love affair with him, have been done with the knowledge that, for the most part, he is unelectable. His candidacy serves one function, and that is to draw public attention and money away from O'Malley, who is, in the eyes of Wall Street, dangerously electable, and whose anti-Wall Street policy goes far beyond Bernie's mere rhetoric.

2. www.counterpunch.org/2015/06/03/why-bernie-sanders-is-a-dead-end/

Creating the Next Presidency

by Robert Ingraham

Feb. 1—As Lyndon LaRouche has made clear, the nomination of either Hillary Clinton or Bernie Sanders by the Democratic Party for the office of U.S. President would be an unparalleled disaster for both the nation and the Democratic Party itself. In an article which accompanies this piece, overwhelming evidence is presented which fleshes out the particulars for Mr. LaRouche's analysis. Whatever her intention might have been during her 2008 campaign for the Presidency, since 2009 Hillary Clinton has sold her soul to Barack Obama. She was personally complicit in many of the crimes of the Obama Administration and remains fiercely subservient to Obama to this day.

Bernie Sanders has repeatedly demonstrated that he is a "non-serious" candidate, a person who is big on talk and short on courage, and whose convictions run a mile wide and an inch deep. He remains an untrustworthy opportunist. At the same time, both Clinton and Sanders are disliked and mistrusted by tens of millions of Americans, and the undeniable reality is that they are both unelectable in the nationwide general election. The nomination of either of them would almost guarantee a Republican Party victory in November, which given the current state of that Party's prospective list of candidates would be a calamity both for the nation and for the entire world. Both Clinton and Sanders must be exposed, discredited, and driven out of the Presidential race as rapidly as possible.

As for Martin O'Malley, Matthew Ogden's presentation in the Jan. 29, 2016 LaRouche PAC National Webcast demonstrated the irrefutable, critically important differences, and the huge moral gulf, which separates O'Malley from both Clinton and Sanders. As Ogden reports, even before the official announcement of his campaign, Martin O'Malley defined the intention behind his decision to run in a guest editorial in the *Des Moines Register* on March 19, 2015. In that article

O'Malley campaigning for the Democratic nomination for President, 2015.

O'Malley stated that "It is time to put the national interest before the interests of Wall Street," and he called for the immediate re-enactment of Franklin Roosevelt's Glass-Steagall legislation. He repeated these themes in the official announcement of his candidacy on May 30, 2015, and as Ogden points out, in the ensuing months O'Malley earned the reputation of Wall Street's "Public Enemy #1."

The issue before the American people is not simply to compare O'Malley, Clinton, and Sanders with each other. The more important truth to be grasped is that we are now facing a breakdown crisis, which threatens economic ruin, chaos, war, and the destruction of the population. As most Americans already sense, we are in a grave crisis, and there is no possibility of escaping this crisis under the current state of affairs. The creation of a new Constitutional Presidency, as the Office of the President was understood by Alexander Hamilton, Abraham Lincoln, and Franklin Roosevelt, is the uniquely required action necessary to overcome the current crisis and avoid a very bleak future.

That potential for a better future exists as a possible future within the O'Malley campaign and within Martin

O'Malley himself. But there are certain things which should be said—and certain lessons from American history which should be noted—at this time.

The Presidency

The office of the U.S. President was created by Alexander Hamilton and his ally Gouverneur Morris at the 1787 Philadelphia Constitutional Convention. Against overwhelming opposition, particularly from the slave states of the South, Hamilton and Morris created a President-led government, one with strong executive powers. Eyewitness reports from that time, as well as statements from Hamilton and Morris themselves, reveal that, of all the issues fought over at the Convention, Hamilton judged the issue of a "Presidential System" to be the most critical, the most indispensable, upon which the viability of the new Republic absolutely rested.

Harper's Weekly/Mathew Brady

Abraham Lincoln on Feb. 27, 1860, the day of his Cooper Union speech.

At the same time, Hamilton and Morris were also responsible for authoring the Constitution's *Preamble* and the inclusion of that Preamble in the final document. It is very clear that, in their creation of the Presidency, it was the intent of Hamilton and Morris to establish an office which would become the guardian of the principles defined in the Preamble, which would embody the historic mission of that Preamble within the person of the President. In other words, the Office of the Presidency was intended to personify the intent of the Constitution and to establish a sacred trust between the President and the people, whereby the President was duty-bound to defend the Constitution and the Republic, and to act on behalf of the people and the nation as a whole.

That is exactly what was accomplished in the first Washington Administration from 1789 to 1793, including most critically the drafting of Alexander Hamilton's Four Reports—commissioned by President Washington—which established an economic system based on the future-oriented physical economic development of the nation, that is, a national Credit System under the sovereign direction of the Nation, as opposed to control by Wall Street speculators such as Aaron Burr.

The American Presidency is an Idea, a Principle, a Mission, oriented toward the future development of the people.[1] The few truly great Presidents in American history have been those who have adopted that mission.

Fighting to Win

As this article goes to press, it is certain that many power brokers in the leadership of the Democratic Party and the news media are telling O'Malley that he "can't win." Perhaps some within the O'Malley camp itself are "crunching the numbers" and concluding that neither the money nor the institutional support is there to successfully contest for the nomination.

In truth, it is Clinton and Sanders who are unelectable, and any hesitation on the part of O'Malley to go all out for the nomination, although perhaps understandable under the circumstances, would be a serious error. Here, again, let us turn to American history.

In 1860 when Abraham Lincoln went into the national Republican Party convention, he was considered by all to be the weakest of the four contenders. No one in the Republican Party leadership expected him to be nominated. Republican Party leaders were lined up behind the two front-runners, William Seward and Salmon Chase. However, Lincoln had already defined a clear national mission for his campaign with his Cooper Union speech (more below), and at the convention his campaign workers labored tirelessly to convince the

---

1. For historical background, see: *The Coming Interim Presidency Under Glass-Steagall: The Name of the Future Is Alexander Hamilton* in *EIR*, July 17, 2015.

delegates that neither Seward nor Chase could win in the general election. They made the point that Lincoln was the one candidate who could win. What seemed impossible became a reality, and Lincoln was nominated on the third ballot.

In January of 1932 Franklin Roosevelt, although he enjoyed a good deal of popular support, was considered a dark horse for the Democratic nomination. Political experts expected the nomination to go once again to Al Smith, the friend of Wall Street and the 1928 nominee. When the Democratic Party convention convened in June, the entirety of the Democratic Party leadership lined up against Roosevelt. Composed primarily of Wall Street allies, these Democratic Party power-brokers bitterly fought Roosevelt's nomination. But earlier that year, with his Forgotten Man Speech (again, more below), Roosevelt had defined a singular mission against the pro-Wall Street Democratic Party leadership. After a fierce convention fight, he was nominated on the fourth ballot.

Franklin Roosevelt campaigns for the Presidency in 1932.

Defining the Mission

To return to Alexander Hamilton's intention for the Presidency—to embody a unified mission to defend the people, the Constitution, and the future development of the nation—it is useful again to consider Lincoln and Roosevelt.

On Feb 27, 1860, Abraham Lincoln delivered his *Cooper Union Speech* in New York City. It was that speech which placed Lincoln at center stage as a national leader. In his remarks, Lincoln was unflinching in his commitment to stop the spread of slavery, to defend the Union, and to save the Republic. This became the mission of his campaign and, as we know today, this mission defined his 1861-1865 Presidency. This was not about "practical politics." Lincoln's address inhabited the realm of moral understanding from which he never departed.

On April 7, 1932, speaking from Albany, New York, Franklin Roosevelt delivered his famous speech, *The Forgotten Man*. It was this speech, and the personal commitment of Roosevelt to the Principle defined in the speech, which propelled him to become a leading contender for the nomination. FDR promised to take on Wall Street and to defend the people of the nation. He

kept his promise, and he never betrayed the American people.

It is worth noting that the principled approach taken by both Lincoln and Roosevelt, far from producing narrow or sectarian campaigns, succeeded in rallying and uniting large numbers of people, across party lines, in enthusiastic support for the candidate's efforts to save the nation. Democrats, Free-Soilers, Know-Nothings, and old Whigs enlisted in Lincoln's cause. In Roosevelt's case, droves of leading Republicans abandoned Herbert Hoover to join with FDR in his fight for the Forgotten Man against Wall Street. When, in 1933, Roosevelt announced his cabinet appointees, several of the leading members, including Henry Wallace and Harold Ickes, were registered Republicans who had joined with him in the fight against Wall Street.

When Lyndon LaRouche advises Martin O'Malley to "stick to the subject," to concentrate on the demand to shut down Wall Street and re-enact Glass-Steagall, this is not simply "practical political advice." What LaRouche is really urging O'Malley to do is what Lincoln did at the Cooper Union in 1860 and what FDR did in Albany in 1932. The people of America are being destroyed. For 15 years, under Bush and Obama, a London/Wall Street financial dictatorship has brought us to the point of ruin. O'Malley must commit himself, without hesitation, to rescuing the nation. Wall Street must be shut down. If O'Malley sticks to that mission, and if he rallies the American people to that mission, the people will respond.

II. Will We Have a Space Program Again, Or Immediate Nuclear War?

KESHA ROGERS

'Genius Is in the Universe and Is Stronger than the Evil We Are Up Against'

Feb. 2—The survival of our nation and that of civilization requires the immediate shutdown of Wall Street and removal of Obama now, to end the death policy of the collapsing and bankrupt trans-Atlantic system. To commit, once again, to the true progress of mankind, we must restore a national commitment to reviving our United States space program. That has been my continued fight, going back six years, when I launched a campaign for the U.S. Congress, calling for the impeachment of Obama for his shutdown of the Constellation program and the dismantling of the manned space program. President Obama has continued to act on behalf of Wall

Kesha Rogers: We must fully restore and fund our space program, so that we can take our part in a "win-win" strategy of cooperation for all nations.

Street and the British Empire, as the chief opposition and as Public Enemy Number One, standing in the way of true scientific progress in this nation.

As a result of that misguided and evil intention, our nation has lost its vision. The people of our nation have been left in grave hopelessness and despair. They have been left with no hope for a future, and have been given a culture that promotes drugs and death. An increased number of our citizens are taking their lives through drugs. People have been left with no real mission, no way of being truly productive.

This course can and must be abolished and a new direction for the progress of mankind must be restored.

That depends on you, the American people, understanding and acting upon the moral advantage which has now been represented through the actions of Russia and China, in particular China, representing a new future for the progress of mankind in space and through a "win-win" strategy of cooperation for all nations. The vision put forth by China and its space program, to explore the far side of the Moon, to be the first to land there, and to do what no nation has yet done, will not just be a great victory for China but for all mankind.

This was the same intention represented by the United States, through the vision and leadership of President John F. Kennedy, when in 1961 he laid before the nation and the world the commitment to land a man on the moon and return him safely to earth.

That vision was only fulfilled six years after President Kennedy was assassinated, but Kennedy's vision was not a one-shot goal. It was the expression of what our nation, and the aspirations of all of mankind, truly represents. It is the idea that all human beings have a common mission to be conquerors in space, to advance mankind's knowledge and understanding of the Universe and the galaxy in which we live. That is the mission that China has dedicated itself to today and one that we in the United States must fully commit ourselves to once again.

Civilization is in danger of being totally obliterated through the unleashing of thermonuclear war, which is now the escalated intention and drive of the British Empire and its puppet Obama, against the nations of Russia and China, the only nations that are representing a leading positive factor throughout the planet, of what mankind can and must become.

Genius is in the universe and is stronger than the evil we are up against.

It was through President Kennedy's vision that a national mission was restored. As Kennedy once declared, "We go in to Space because whatever mankind must undertake, free men must fully share."

That commitment to true freedom has been lost. It was lost with the death of President Kennedy and the capitulation to a degenerate culture. The loss of the obligation and dedication to a national science-driver mission, and the abolition of a national mission in space,

has been the result of turning our space program over to the hands of the Wall Street monetarists, budget cutters, and the anti-human, anti-science, environmentalist agenda.

In 2011 China laid out its mission for achievement in the exploration of both the moon and space. The preface or statement of principle that was put forth at that time states, "Outer space is the common wealth of mankind. Exploration, development and utilization of outer space are an unremitting pursuit of mankind."

As many know the old saying, "Where there is no vision the people will perish," so today, we must no longer leave the people of our nation and the world to perish under the destructive hand of Obama and Wall Street. We have a choice—to join with China in fulfilling the truly creative intentions of mankind. Our space program must be fully restored and funded. We must inspire the people of this nation once again that they have something great to live for, and that they can, once again, take pride in being truly productive contributors to progress throughout this nation and throughout the world.

Only a Scientific and Cultural Renaissance Can Stop the Dark Age Now Descending Upon Humanity

by Helga Zepp-LaRouche

Jan. 26—Helga Zepp-LaRouche addressed an EIR Forum at the National Press Club on Jan. 26. What follow are edited excerpts from her remarks. She was preceded by Thomas Wysmuller, a former NASA meteorologist, who refuted the claim that atmospheric carbon dioxide influences climate, which he develops fully here. The discussion following the two presentations, excerpted below, emphasized the vital importance of the space program, which was further defunded by Obama.

I will try to be brief. Obviously, the question is, how is such a report as you just discussed possible? Why? What is the motive? Why would you go through the effort of falsifying data and trying to squash an honest debate among scientists? And I think once you pursue that question to the end, you would come to the conclusion of my presentation, which I want to state at the beginning: that the entire trans-Atlantic region—and I'm fully aware where I'm saying this; namely, in Washington D.C.—is run by very destructive policies and very destructive forces.

Now, let me start with a point which should be of the biggest concern of anybody who wants to live out his lifespan; and that is that we are on the verge of thermonuclear war. And contrary to the height of the Cold War, during the Cuban Missile Crisis, or at other high points of the Cold War where people were concerned about the possible extinction of mankind, even though we are much closer to it, there is no public concern, there is no public debate about it. And only rare individuals, such as former Defense Secretary William Perry, or nuclear specialist Hans Kristensen, are warning of the possibility that the world could go to war.

Now, if you want to take it on the light side, the

Helga Zepp-LaRouche (center) and Thomas Wysmuller (left) at the EIR Forum on Jan. 26, at the National Press Club. Forum moderator Michael Billington is at right.

danger of accidental war is extremely high, simply because the normal kind of code of behavior, which existed even between Kennedy and Khrushchov is presently not there. After the Ukraine crisis exploded, the NATO-Russian consultations—an institution which was created to be there in times of crisis—were cancelled and abandoned.

However, I would take it a step further to say that the evolution of military doctrines in NATO, going from Mutually Assured Destruction (MAD) to the idea of a winnable first strike posture is based on a series of global war doctrines and capabilities which all point in the direction of such a possibility. Key features of the winnable first-strike nuclear war strategy include:
- The missile defense system around the world;
- The Prompt Global Strike;
- The Air-Sea Battle doctrine against China;
- The modernization of nuclear weapons in Europe.

In the face of these developments, Russia and China have drawn their conclusions and they are basically also gearing up their arsenals. William Perry warned just a couple of days ago in the *Boston Globe*, that we are far advanced into a new arms race with nuclear weapons. $1 trillion will be spent on the nuclear buildup over the next 30 years, according to President Obama. Given the condition of the world financial system, this sounds a little bit ludicrous, but this bears out the danger.

And if it comes to a war, by intention because some people have the illusion that you can win a nuclear war, or by accident; I think civilization very well may not exist within minutes, hours, or at the latest weeks. A nuclear winter would evolve, and that would possibly be the end of civilization. And all the beautiful things mankind has accomplished so far would be in vain: There would be nobody to even comment on it. No historian, nobody making an archive on it; not even a museum. So that is the one danger.

Systemic Breakdown Crisis

The other danger which is in direct correlation with the war danger is the fact that the trans-Atlantic financial system is about to blow up in much bigger ways than the crisis of 2007-2008. As you know, the World Economic Forum in just took place in Davos, where people officially went through the usual kind of eclectic series of entertainment on different subjects; but behind closed doors or among themselves privately there was an absolute panic.

And publicly it was expressed by the former chief economist of the Bank for International Settlements, William White, who gave an interview to the *Daily Telegraph*, in which he said that since nothing has been done to re-regulate the banking system since 2008, the world indebtedness today is so large that this debt can neither be repaid nor serviced. He added that people who think they own a lot of money in this virtual world of finance may wake up to very unpleasant surprises: Namely, that it could evaporate in one minute.

What were the measures, the so-called "tool box," which the financial institutions came up with after the 2008 Lehman Brothers/AIG crisis? It was quantitative easing, it was bail-outs, it was various kinds of measures to basically turn private gambling debt into public state debt. Therefore, you now have a state debt crisis. The recent developments which came in with Dodd-Frank and the legislation in the EU Commission are to go for bail-in solutions, which they call the Cyprus model.

This happened three years ago in Cyprus, where banks basically went bankrupt and then the banks confiscated the amounts of money in the accounts of either people who had their savings there, or had shares of the banks, or were holding bonds. And these holdings were basically expropriated by 50%.

Jeroen Dijsselbloem, the Finance Minister of Holland, who is also the head of the Eurogroup, at that time said this Cyprus model is the blueprint for the entire Eurozone; and legislation was enacted. As I said, Dodd-Frank, Article II in the United States has that provision; all the European governments made legislation in the meantime to go for that. But the problem is—and this was just noted by Thomas Hoenig, who is the vice chairman of the FDIC in the United States, and similarly an unnamed EU official gave an interview to Reuters just three days ago—saying the problem is, this bail-in does not function; the banks have not been re-capitalized enough to do it, and so they are not prepared. And furthermore, the amount which you could generate if you bailed in all the accounts—business, private people—and go for additional bail-out measures, you would get approximately $18-20 trillion; the problem is, the outstanding derivative debt is about $2 quadrillion.

William White says this debt will never be paid, and we have to have what he calls a Jubilee, pointing to the fact that in all great religions over the last 5,000 years, you had periodic debt write-offs when it became clear it was not payable. So, Mr. White is now a high-ranking

UNHCR/I. Brickett

A Syrian refugee family that crossed the Aegean Sea to Greece in an overcrowded and leaking vessel.

member of the Organization for Economic Co-operation (OECD), as well as the former chief economist for the Bank for International Settlements, and you can call it a Jubilee, you can call it a debt conference to write down this debt, or you can call it Glass-Steagall.

Now, that's just two of the situations on the financial front. But we are now reaching a breaking point in trans-Atlantic civilization. Let me emphasize two other aspects of why we are in a decaying, collapsing, destructive society both in the United States and in Europe.

In the United States, apart from the abysmal collapse of real production, you have a drug epidemic which was highlighted by several articles in the *New York Times* in the last several weeks, based on a study from Princeton, and another one from the CDC.

These studies show that shockingly, the death rate in the United States for white males in all age groups is increasing to such an extent that it outweighs and erases the progress in medicine. In the age group of white Americans—not black, not Hispanic, but white Americans—between 24 and 35, the death rates from suicide, alcoholism, or drug overdose has increased 500%. There is presently in all 3007 counties of the United States, an increase, a doubling or quadrupling of the suicide rate; there are 125 people per day committing suicide or dying from drug overdoses. That is five people per hour; so, since we have been here, five people have died. It's one every 12 minutes, and it is a

sign of a dying society. This increase has happened since 2001, and you can think for yourself which Presidencies have been in charge since then. And just from that figure, you can conclude that you do not have good government in the United States.

The European Crisis

In Europe, on the other hand, we have a slightly different problem. We have a refugee crisis, which is detonating the EU. As you know, last year there were almost one million refugees who arrived primarily from Syria and from Iraq. But now, the arrivals include many people from Afghanistan and from Northern Africa. And at the Davos conference, the director of Davos, Kurt Schwab, said that he thinks that if the present oil price collapse is not stopped, there will soon be 1 billion people coming to the shores of Europe; and I think that that is not an exaggeration at all.

Of course, the causes of this refugee crisis are the failed policies of the British and of the United States: The failed wars based on:

- Lies in Iraq, in Afghanistan, in Libya;
- The attempt to topple Assad in Syria;
- The war in Yemen.

And has any of this served the interest of the United States? I don't think so; I think it has damaged the United States and the reputation of the United States around the world.

Now, as you know, Chancellor Merkel has done something right: she said we welcomed these people. And she's being criticized a lot for it. But at the moment when she said that, there was no other way, because you had thousands and tens of thousands of people being stuck in the Balkans between Macedonia, Croatia, and Hungary, because Hungary began to build a wall around its borders. So, it was a humanitarian crisis of unbelievable dimensions; and there is such a thing as an asylum right guaranteed by the Geneva Convention, and by the UN Charter. So Merkel did the right thing, she did the right thing concerning the refugees; but obviously you have to change policy if you want to accommodate these refugees.

The result of the non-solidarity of the EU, is that all of Eastern Europe refuses to take one single refugee; the foreign minister of Austria just yesterday blasted

Greece for not enforcing the security of the outer border of the EU. And the Greek government very correctly said, "What do they want us to do? Do they want us to shoot the refugees in their boats and drive them back into the ocean?"

And you all have seen these horrendous pictures where small children are caught between soldiers and barbed wire, razor wire. If this is not resolved in a human way, this is the moral end of Europe; and anybody who is any good has understood that perfectly well.

However, fortunately, this is not the totality of the picture. Because you have right now, two universes: You have the trans-Atlantic world which is collapsing, and you have a completely different kind of political system emerging, coming primarily from China. And don't believe any China-bashing which you have read in the *Washington Post* or the *New York Times*.

I have been monitoring developments in China for the better part of 45 years or so, and I can assure you that China right now is not only an economic miracle; the purported news about the so-called Chinese stock exchange collapse triggering all these problems in the Atlantic world is complete nonsense, because the real economy of China is doing excellently, and you will see in the second half of 2016, that all the many, many investments in real economy—Xi Jinping was just on a trip to the Middle East; he went to Saudi Arabia, Iran, and Egypt. The total volume of investments is between 55 and 100 billion, only including these three countries. And if you look at the large amount of Chinese investments in many, many countries, in Latin America, in Asia, in Africa, in Eastern Europe,— you will see that that will be an economic engine which will remain there for the next several years.

However, even more important, China, a little bit more than two years ago, offered a fundamentally new policy: the New Silk Road. Now, the New Silk Road is the idea, in the tradition of the ancient Silk Road of the Han Dynasty of 2,000 years ago, to further economic cooperation, scientific exchange of ideas, cultural exchange, and to promote a new infrastructure integration of the whole planet. I think that this has affected the policy of the BRICS; it is right now moving forward very quickly, and you have a strategic partnership of China, Russia, India, and many countries cooperating closely. Such as, for example, now between China

creative commons/James Grellier

A Middle East reconstruction program for real development will require extensive desalination of sea water. Here, a reverse osmosis desalination plant in Barcelona, Spain.

and Iran. You have an increased activity along these lines among many countries, including China and Greece; China and East European countries that turned to China to have fast train systems built by China; and many investments in Africa and in other areas of the world.

Now, should that be regarded as a threat by the United States? Only if you believe that the maintenance of a unipolar world is the only way to go, at a point when a multipolar world is already a reality. The idea that there has to be a unipolar world and that you have to eliminate, through regime change, every country in the world which does not submit to such an order,— is the guarantee that we will blow ourselves up as a civilization. What China has offered—Xi Jinping offered that to President Obama at the APEC meeting in 2014, in Beijing; he offered to cooperate with the United

States and other major powers in a "win-win" cooperation, to transform the world economy.

The Land-Bridge Policy

Now, to my knowledge Obama has not answered that. But this is now becoming a realistic possibility, because we have published this report, "The New Silk Road Becomes the World Land-Bridge": Because we have been working on this New Silk Road policy since the collapse of the Soviet Union. This was our answer to the fall of the Berlin Wall in Germany, to the end of the Iron Curtain. We proposed in '91, to connect Europe and Asia through so-called "infrastructure corridors." And we have campaigned for this policy for 25 years, and therefore, we were naturally extremely happy when Xi Jinping in 2013 said the New Silk Road is now the Chinese policy. As a matter of fact, we said that is exactly how we will get out of this mess.

And then, we started to make our report. This is a map of all the corridors, bridges, and tunnels which will eventually unite all the continents of the world, and bring unity to all the different development areas of the planet.

So we have said, since 2012 at the latest, that the *only* way that you will end terrorism in the Middle East and bring peace to this tortured region of the world, is you have to have—I hate to call it a "Marshall Plan," because "Marshall Plan" always has the connotation of a Cold War dimension to it—but just to use the word so that people get an idea that there have been examples of successful reconstruction of war-torn regions. I would like to call it the extension of the Silk Road to the Middle East, which is already uniting Central Asia. It's moving into South Asia; a corridor is being built by China through Pakistan to the Persian Gulf. In 2012, we held a conference in Frankfurt proposing a Silk Road Marshall Plan for Southwest Asia, the Middle East, the Near East, and Africa, as the only way that you can end terrorism.

Terrorism has now become a menace: We have seen it in Paris, twice last year; the *Charlie Hebdo* massacre, then the horrible massacre in Paris later in the year; there have been terrorist events all over the planet, practically in all countries.

Will you be able to stop this horror show by bombing ISIS or al-Qaeda? Well, you have to do something. And I think the best approach right now is what has been negotiated by Secretary of State John Kerry together with [Russian Foreign Minister] Sergei Lavrov in the Vienna conference, which was very successful in getting Saudi Arabia, Iran, Turkey, and other parties of the Middle East at one table. The resumption of this conference was delayed because there were still some tensions, because Saudi Arabia didn't want certain opposition groups from Syria; the Turks didn't want the Kurds; but, I think that Russia, the United States, China, and the other major powers of the Middle East must sit together and say "we will militarily eliminate ISIS, but then you need something else."

You need a reconstruction program which gives real hope to the people in the Middle East of drying up the environment from which al-Qaeda and al-Nusra, and ISIS have been recruiting. And it will work *only* if you put a Marshall Plan, a Silk Road Marshall Plan into the region, where all these countries,— Russia, China, India, Iran, Egypt, Germany, Italy, France, the United States,— work together and say: We will take the entire region from the Caucasus to the Persian Gulf, from Afghanistan to the Mediterranean, as one region, and we will put in real development. We declare a war on the desert; we will create new water! If you have ever flown over that region, this is all desert. There is not one little oasis—nothing!

So you need to have large amounts of ocean water desalinated, which is only possible through nuclear energy; you need to tap into the moisture in the atmosphere, which you can do through ionization. You can use aquifers and other methods. And then you can develop agriculture. You can develop forestry.

You have to put in infrastructure; infrastructure as dense as it is, for example, in Germany. Germany is a perfect example of a very well-developed infrastructural country. Then you can put in new cities, you can build industries.

And then you will give the people of the region a new hope. A hope that they can have a future, that they can become engineers, that they can become scientists, that it's worthwhile to have a family. And that is how you bring peace to the Middle East and to Africa.

I have said this in many speeches, and people have said this is completely utopian. Who should pay for this? I believe that if you have a breakdown of an old paradigm and if you have a good plan, I believe that then you can be successful, simply because you are the only one who has the right idea. And I am totally flabbergasted and surprised, but I have to announce that one of the persons in Germany, who is not—and I emphasize *not*—on my favorite list, Wolfgang Schäuble, is now coming out for a Marshall Plan in the Middle East!

He did that in a very surprising speech in Davos, where, to the surprise of everybody, he said, "well, it should be obvious that we have to invest many billions in the region, that we have to form a 'coalition of the willing' to do so," in a beautiful reversal of the coalition of the willing of Bush, you know, who wanted it to make war; so Schäuble, of all people, now wants to have a "coalition of the willing" to reconstruct the Middle East. And this is now being picked up by newspapers in Germany.

The Evolution of Mankind

And you know, I always said, when there is no reason you can appeal to, the only thing which causes political change, is what I call the "policy of the burning shirt." That when people realize that their shirt is getting a little bit hot on their behind, they start to move. And I can assure you, this refugee crisis right now, is exactly that, because the EU is about to detonate. If they build, again, borders around each country, then the Schengen Agreement is out of the window, and everybody is now saying openly that if there is no Schengen Agreement, then the European Monetary Union doesn't make any sense; the Eurozone will collapse; and very likely also the EU. Because then you will have no *raison d'être* any longer for this alliance, as it developed from Maastricht to Lisbon.

So I think we now have a tremendous situation. I think we need to have a change in paradigm. I think people have to recognize,— and you may not believe what I'm saying, but I want you to think about it,— that if we stay in the old paradigm of geopolitical confrontation, with Russia, with China, the likelihood that we will not exist as a civilization is very high.

If, however, we look at the longer arc of the evolution of mankind,— mankind has been only around for a short time, a few million years. The record in terms of writing and other readable artifacts is, maybe 10,000 years. And just think what a tremendous development mankind has made in the last 10,000 years, from the Stone Age, where you would use a stone to kill your neighbor; now you have a smart phone of the same size; you can have international conferences, you see the people you're talking to around the globe. And in 10,000 years, people will say, "Oh, these people with their 'smart phones,' they thought that was already a big accomplishment," because they will be communicating from one galaxy to the other, and look back at our period as the "Stone Age."

So you have to have a tremendous sense of opti-

We must combine economic reconstruction with a renaissance of Classical culture and a dialogue of the highest phases of all cultures. Here, a modern statue of Chandragupta Maurya (340-c. 297 BC) at the Laxminarayan Temple in Delhi, India. His rule, renowned for its thriving agriculture, trade, art, and architecture, was followed by more advanced phases of high culture, including especially that of the Gupta Empire, at its zenith from about 240 to 550 AD.

mism in mankind. Mankind is the only species which can, again and again, change the knowledge about the physical universe, making discoveries, and I believe that there is a limitless ability for mankind to improve, both intellectually and morally. I don't think that people have to be as mean as they are right now. I don't think that the drug culture, with all the ugliness that goes along with it, is what should be the worthiness of man.

I think that if we combine an economic reconstruction program with a cultural Renaissance, that we will go into a completely new era of civilization where man will be truly man! Truly beautiful! We have written an addendum to this report which is called "The United States Joins the New Silk Road."

It advances the idea that the Silk Road should not only be built in China and Africa, but the United States urgently needs a Silk Road-style development. Has the United States a fast train system? I don't think so. Has the United States a functioning airplane system? I think it's getting a little bit shabby and old.

So why not build 50,000 km, or 35,000 miles of maglev train or other high-speed train systems, connecting the East Coast, the West Coast, the North and the South; reconstruct some of the cities which are falling apart; build some new cities!—some beautiful cities in the South; inspire people to go back to the Moon, rebuild NASA to go to Mars just to find out why the universe is built the way it is!

This problem of the Sun is very urgent, because in 2 billion years the Sun will not make it so comfortable on the planet Earth,— so we have think how we as a species can live on as a species in the Galaxy and beyond.

So I think what we need to do, is we have to have an honest, fearless discussion about the change of a paradigm. And I think we have to recognize that good government also means to have a beautiful culture which uplifts people. I named the Schiller Institute, "Schiller Institute," because I believe that the image of man of Friedrich Schiller is the most beautiful I have found on the planet. And he basically said, Art is only art if it is beautiful and if it ennobles people.

So we need to combine this economic reconstruction with a Classical Renaissance of Classical culture, and then start a dialogue of the high phases of all cultures: Confucianism in China, which fortunately has a Renaissance right now, which has the whole country excited; people in China are completely optimistic. They believe in the government—can you imagine that? They have trust in the government? So, they're in a good shape. China has produced beautiful poetry, painting, as well as Mencius and other great neo-Confucian thinkers.

India has produced many high points: The Gupta period. The Arab world was once in much better shape during the Abbasid Dynasty, when Baghdad was the cultural capital of the world. You had the Italian Renaissance, you had the Andalusian Renaissance. If we revive all of these high points of cultures, I'm absolutely certain that we can create a new Renaissance of human civilization, this time on a completely different set of axioms than those of the present decaying trans-Atlantic world.

But I think, if you think about it, we are on the verge of calamity beyond belief. But we can turn it around if we go back to FDR policies, Glass-Steagall, shut down Wall Street, make a new credit system, get production going. And it will be easy. [applause]

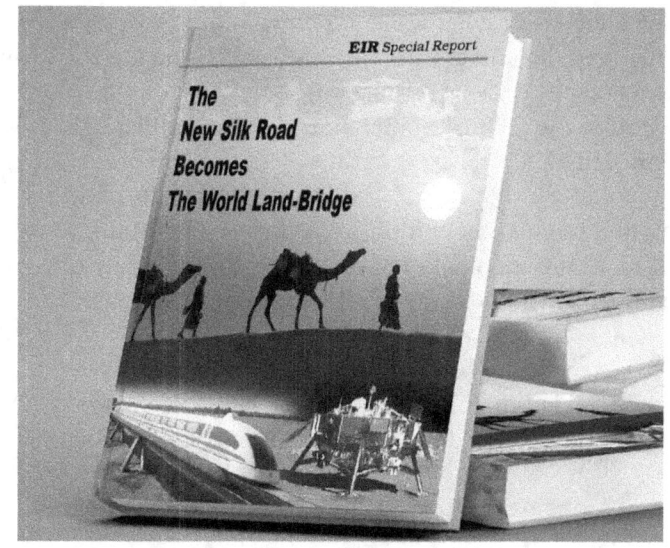

'I'm Absolutely Optimistic that Mankind Has the Possibility To Dramatically Change'

Jan. 26—This is a transcript of the dialogue between the speakers at the Jan. 26, 2016 EIR forum at the National Press Club, Helga Zepp-LaRouche and Tom Wysmuller, and members of the audience.

Tom Wysmuller: [in response to the presentation by Helga Zepp-LaRouche] Helga, if I can add, if we stop wasting *billions* on climate research, you can buy a lot of bricks for that New Silk Road.

Michael Billington: I can assure you, the Chinese are not wasting much of their money.

So I want to open the floor to questions in just a moment. First, I want to say that when you do leave, we have copies of this report, *The New Silk Road Becomes the World Land-Bridge* for which Helga was the inspiration. She has a long introduction; it's a 370 page, detailed analysis of what we could do with the world as a whole, and the universe, if we could overcome the political insanity now governing our society.

Before the COP21 conference, we also published a report called "'Global Warming' Scare Is Population Reduction, Not Science." Half of it is an analysis of how this population control movement—this Malthusian idea of depopulation—was fostered on behalf of the oligarchy, such as the royal families in London and Holland.

The second half is, as Tom was talking about, *real* science, real climate science. We hope to have some of the material Tom's done included in our publications later.

Let's open the floor for questions to both of our speakers.

Visas for al-Qaeda

Question: I'm Mike Springmann. I'm not sure whether I have a question or a couple of statements. I would dispute the analysis of the Middle East, based on my book, *Visas for al-Qaeda: CIA Handouts That Rocked the World*. It basically talked about how the United States has created an organized terrorist group, that once was the mujahideen, then was rebranded as al-Qaeda, and is now rebranded as ISIL. And the problems with the Middle East stem from the United States and its repressive allies in the area, recruiting arming, financing, and training these people.

And they were carefully connected, I think, to be driven into Europe, through Turkey, another one of America's repressive allies, and Frau Merkel said, "Y'all come," and they did! There'd been a steady trickle in the past from North Africa, thanks to America's Libya policies. But now it's North Africa, the Middle East, and all over the world. And they're in Germany, they're welcomed with opened arms; from what I can see, the hope of driving down wages, or at least preventing them from rising. They will be used to split the natives apart from one another; they will be used to create hate between the Christian Europeans and the Muslims and the Arabs, which has been done.

We've seen how Germany and France and Britain have been driven into the American war in the Middle East. The French started bombing Syria—they sent an aircraft carrier, the nuclear-powered *Charles de Gaulle*; Germany sent two frigates to the Mediterranean, the *Augsburg* and *Karlsruhe*, one of which was an escort to the *Charles de Gaulle* carrier which is bombing Syria and Iraq. And I think it's a complete disaster and I think it's basically American policy.

This is being aided and abetted by the German chancellor, who really ought to know better. From what I've seen, it's a disaster, and it's getting worse. You had carefully coordinated robberies, rapes, and thefts of cellphones and gropings, all throughout Germany on New Year's Eve, and Manuel Ochsenreiter, who is the publisher of *Zuerst!* an online magazine among other things, showed a video of Berlin with the caption, "This is not Berlin in April of 1945, this is Berlin on New Year's Eve 2015." And it's all of the aliens firing strictly controlled handguns into the air, and shooting rockets and roman candles, horizontally into the crowd. And the German government did nothing!

In Cologne, the lord mayor refused to take any action and said everyone should keep an arm's length from strangers, to avoid being raped, and when a thousand protesters came out the next week, about her policies, a water cannon was turned on them.

The color revolution in Ukraine: troops of the Azov Batallion. "Were seeing that something similar is starting right now in Moldova! When does this stop?!"

So, anyway, I'm talking too much. Read my book *Visas for al-Qaeda*, it pretty much sets forth the basis for current policy.

Helga Zepp-LaRouche: I think you're mixing obviously truthful facts with a view of the matter which doesn't give any hope. And I'm talking about how to get out of this situation.

I could give you a several-hour presentation on how the United States policy, starting with Brzezinski in 1975, in Tokyo, proposed to play the "Islamic card," how that was used to build up the mujahideen in Afghanistan against the Soviet Union; how that evolved into what you are correctly saying, including what happened in Libya, in Benghazi; and you know, General Michael Flynn has said the same thing. He said that he briefed the White House that they were planning a caliphate, and that he thought the White House had an intention to allow that to happen—all of that is true!

I didn't want to go at length into the known history of how this disaster happened, and I agree with you, it is a horrible disaster!

How Do We Get Out of This?

However, the question is, how do we get out of this? Consider how we got into this crisis. Many people warned about this danger, including the former U.S. ambassador to Moscow at the time of the collapse of the Soviet Union, Jack Matlock. In addition, you had such people as Horst Teltschik and many others who were eyewitnesses, who said that Russia had been promised that NATO would not expand to the borders of Russia. And then, unfortunately, you had the policy of the Project for the New American Century, the PNAC doctrine. basically, from the beginning, you had a policy of regime change, of color revolutions, of Victoria Nuland. They have said publicly that they have spent $5 billion in Ukraine alone, to build all these NGOs and so forth for regime change, first with the Orange Revolution in 2004, and then the whole Maidan coup.

And you know, given the fact that I have a positive conception of what the world should look like, I follow events more critically in making evaluations, because I see what they are detrimental to. And therefore, when the EU made the association offer to Ukraine in November 2013, it was very clear that this was a provocation which would eventually mean that NATO would have access to the Black Sea, and even American think tanks like Stratfor had long articles saying that that was unacceptable from a Russian standpoint, because of the location of the Russian Black Sea Fleet, and the relatively indefensible danger of NATO being only 300 km away from Moscow.

So it was very clear that the decision by Yanukovych not to sign that EU agreement was an admittedly late recognition that this agreement wouldn't work. In addition, it would have opened up Russia to cheap products from the European Union (EU). So, who is responsible for the Ukraine crisis, therefore?

Maastricht Led to the Maidan

I fully agree with what the late German Chancellor Helmut Schmidt said: The Ukraine crisis started with the Maastricht agreement.

Maastricht was the turning point at which the EU was transformed from a European alliance into an imperial, expansionist movement, trying to expand eastward. And they would like to expand as far as they possibly could, according to the words of Robert Cooper, who was the adviser of Lady Ashton [then the EU foreign policy representative].

Then, of course, you had the Maidan, which was immediately subverted by the Bandera groupings, who were old Nazis who were kept by by MI6, the CIA, and by the German Intelligence BND/Gehlen organization during the Cold War. So these were known entities, and nobody can tell me that the Western governments didn't know what they were dealing with during the Nazi coup in Ukraine!

So if you look at the question, how did we come to this point?, you have the NATO expansion to the Russian border; you now have provocations everywhere. So you have to understand that Russia is not the evil one. And I'm fully aware that in Washington there is a prevailing view that Russia is the culprit, that Putin is a monster; I can assure you that, if it were not for Russia, we probably would have had World War III already! And the fact that Russia has now moved in a *brilliant* way in Syria, basically taking back large areas from ISIS by supporting the legitimate government of Assad. There is such a *spin* put on the chronology of these events and who committed the atrocity and what was the reaction! And that is the logic of war: Once you are in a war, all sides commit crimes. There has not been one war where that didn't happen.

What I'm saying is that Germany and France and Italy were drawn into this Cold War provocation of sanctions against Russia. This is very much to the detriment of German interests, because German industry is losing more than Russia! Russia can go to China and elsewhere, but Germany is losing export markets forever! So that was very dangerous. And I'm extremely happy, that there was a change after the intervention of

ISIS fighters in Yarmouk, near Damascus, Syria. "As long as you have Wahhabism, and the Salafist idea to eradicate culture, you will have new groups. If ISIS is eradicated, there will be a new group!"

Putin in Syria. There was also a change because the refugee crisis forced Germany to say, "wait a second, we cannot solve this problem without Russia." So therefore you have now, amazingly, German Finance Minister Wolfgang Schäuble, who is not my favorite man—I said it again—is welcoming the Russian deployment in Syria, as is the German Foreign Minister Frank-Walter Steinmeier, and various other people.

Quarantine Wahhabism

This is a good thing, because if you get an agreement among the people who are participating in the Vienna congress, to militarily reconquer Syria and Iraq, you can get rid of ISIS; ISIS is not that many people. But then, you have to do something to change the environment, because the evolution from the mujahideen to al-Qaeda to al-Nusra to ISIS shows that as long as you have Wahhabism, and the Salafist idea of eradicating culture, you will have new groups. If ISIS is eradicated, there will be a new group!

And I'm talking about a *thorough*,— an immediate and thorough solution to dry out terrorism for sure. I have said this many times: If you have the power of the United States, Russia, China, and India, that alone is enough to put these other countries in containment. Because what would Saudi Arabia be without the United States? Nothing.

You can change the rules. If the big powers can be gotten at one table and work together, we can solve it.

And it's the only human thing to do. Realize that we are about to lose our humanity: Look at this drug epidemic in the United States, and look at people like German Deputy Finance Minister Jens Spahn, who said, "Oh, we shouldn't be afraid of ugly pictures, when we deport women and children back to the countries they come from." I don't think we will morally survive that. We are about to lose our humanity.

A New Paradigm

Instead I'm proposing that these programs are a way to change to a new paradigm, and I'm absolutely optimistic that mankind has the possibility to dramatically change. If you look at the change from the Middle Ages, which was dominated by scholasticism, by peripatetics, by witchcraft, by all kinds of horror-shows, but then you had the Renaissance, you have Nicholas of Cusa, you had Brunelleschi, you had great minds which created the new paradigm which created modern times and which had a completely different set of axioms.

What I'm saying is that we need a change of axioms as fundamental as the change from the Middle Ages to modern times, if we want to survive.

Question: Hello, my name is V—B—. I didn't catch the book author's name, but I thought he brought up some very important points. Because as you were speaking—and this is all very interesting and very relevant—you just said something about, for example, the images of refugees being sent back, the children and the mothers, that we're losing our humanity, but we stand to lose a great deal more if we don't stem the tide of this ludicrous refugee crisis, which was precipitated on fictitious premises. Because you have mentioned in the last couple of minutes that there are people who are suggesting that the refugee crisis could get to the point where there are some billions of people coming from Iraq, and Afghanistan, and northern Africa, and Syria into Europe.

And at the same time, you also mentioned that the whole paradigm, the whole philosophical international viewpoint of nuclear war has changed since the '60s. It used to be that we understood it was a potential mutual destruction, whereas now we're thinking it's a winnable situation. Well, if you have on the one hand, a billion refugees coming in, and completely changing the population of Europe, who's going to be behind the nuclear buttons in just another 10 or 20 years?

No More Color Revolutions!

So we can worry about losing our humanity, but I think we stand to lose a great deal more if we don't stem the tide of these refugees. And I therefore think that as important as it is to look forward, you can't look forward without also looking back. We have to step backwards and look at what really precipitated the refugee crisis. The gentleman brought up the rise, going from the Taliban, to al-Qaeda, to ISIS, and the United States' role in this, and it's very important to take a look at that, because if we don't examine how it started then—these color revolutions, for example, that are leadership deposals in so many countries, which are creating the power vacuums into which these so-called rebels groups begin to run like cockroaches that, as soon as the light is off, and they're in there and they're reproducing! But if we're going to continue to destroy the power structures in countries like Syria, whose leader we're trying so hard to remove, and completely ignoring what happened after we did this in Iraq and in Libya for God's sake!

You know, we created a situation where these people are developing strength; you know, we pay for the people, for example, that we think are going to serve our purposes in a given country, and someone comes along, they sell some illegal oil, they have more money and they just run over to the other side.

So we have to look back, we have to stop these ridiculous color revolutions, and leadership deposals, and let the leadership in a given nation stay there! It's none of the United States' call to decide who should be running Syria. I think we should step back and let Assad keep his country intact. We've already seen what, God knows what happened, in Libya.

So it's very important to examine, what are we doing wrong? I mean, you mentioned also the Ukraine and Victoria Nuland, admitting that we spent some $5 billion and upwards of regime change money over in the Ukraine! We're seeing that something similar is starting to happen right now in Moldova! When does this stop?!

I don't see how we can maintain a concern for humanity and culture, if we're decimating country after country after country. So we definitely have to start a conversation about what we *did* wrong, so that we can get the United States, the American people, to see that we have to stop doing this, and stop having Ted Cruz and people send around their surveys for Presidential support, saying "Don't you think we should be—do you agree with me that the United States should lead the charge against ISIS?" In other words, what he's trying to say is, don't you think we should send our troops and get them on the ground in Syria.

We need a conversation about this. Because we *are* one of the main problems, and only a change in our conversation is going to wake up the American people so that we can just let the rest of the world live, and culture continue.

Danger of Nuclear War

Zepp-LaRouche: I couldn't agree with you more, and I'm very happy that you seem to be a full, red-blooded American, ... compared to the blue-bloods. [laughter]

No, I agree with you. And there was a letter just put out, an open letter to the American people by Richard Falk and a couple of other people, pointing to the war danger, saying that it is an absolute scandal that none of the Presidential candidates has even touched the issue. And that's why I put the danger of nuclear war at the beginning of my remarks, because, not to say that these other crises are not equally existential, but if this happens, it would be the end.

There must be a public discussion, is it the right thing to entertain the idea that nuclear war is winnable? And I have read enough articles by all the experts, commenting on this, that I think there is no question that there are people who think you can win a nuclear war, including a limited nuclear war in Europe. Why would you modernize nuclear weapons in Europe? The B61-12 bomb, which is supposed to be so small and so smooth, and a bunker buster—and you know, there is no debate about that! And I can only encourage you, we must discuss that. Is it legitimate to plan for nuclear war? Isn't that a Nuremberg Crime? Isn't it an absolute insanity to maintain nuclear weapons when that implies the possible extinction of civilization?

I fully agree: Let's have this debate and have it a lot. We have had previous events where we discussed this—every Friday we have a webcast where these issues are being raised. But the reason why I wanted the idea of a future orientation, is because I think we are now at a moment where the situation can be changed only if people, including the Americans, see a positive idea of the future. Consider, why do so many Ameri-

creative commons/wikiHow

"There are people who think you can win a nuclear war," such as Herman Kahn, Albert Wohlstetter, and the Pentagons Office of Net Assessment. Here, some of their propaganda on a wikiHow page titled, "How to Survive a Nuclear Attack." The page has been visited more than a million times.

cans commit suicide? Now, that should shock people! It should shock the hell out of people that Americans are killing themselves more quickly than medicine makes progress in curing diseases! If that is not a symptom of a dying society, I don't know what is.

And how do you get hope? We have to do what Franklin D. Roosevelt did with the Civilian Conservation Corps, the CCC program: The same young people who are now despairing in drug addiction must be brought into—we have to build America. We have here now, a first study about how you can rebuild the United States. And that's what FDR would do. FDR would close down Wall Street; he would put in a Pecora Commission and put all these bankers in jail, because the banks are laundering the money of the Mexico drug cartel. HSBC laundered in one year, I think $100 billion in drug money from Mexico alone, and then they got a $1.9 billion fine. They had already calculated that into the operating costs! It's a tiny amount of money.

All the Afghanistan heroin, you know, the various anti-drug czars, like Antonio Maria Costa from the United Nations, or Viktor Ivanov, said the entire financial system would have already collapsed but for the influx of the drug money.

So Wall Street has to be scrutinized and we have to see—you know, the LIBOR manipulation, the drug money laundering—you have a criminal banking system, but nobody went to jail!

So, anyway, we could have many, many of such things, but I welcome what you're saying.

Question: G— R—: First of all, I want to note that Concepción, who for 30 years sat over in front of the White House on the sidewalk protesting the idea of nuclear war, passed away yesterday. So that protest, that continuous 24/7/365 protest for the last 30 years, is gone now.

Anyway, I very much appreciated your proposing that we're facing an existential threat to our humanity. That's very profound and very far-reaching, and I hope you can get that concept circulated. The whole idea of our very existence is a big part of the Zionist-imperialism stuff. Their fear, their sense that they are existentially threatened when they're existentially threatening so many others.

But I wanted to address the question of taking the profit out of war. We seem to be—certainly this city—is run by the war profiteers. It seems our government is run by the war profiteers, and so I'm wondering what you might have to say with regard to that?

China's President Xi at a joint press conference with President Obama at the White House, Sept. 25, 2015. President Xi's Three No's for China: "No interference in the internal affairs of other nations. No attempt to increase the so-called 'sphere of influence.' No striving for hegemony or dominance." President Obama's three no's for the world: No end to war. No industrial development. No interference with British imperial hegemony.

Bullet Trains, Not Bullets

Zepp-LaRouche: I don't know if it was [former] Defense Secretary William Perry, or one of the other experts, who said that the announcement by President Obama of the plan to spend $1 trillion in the modernization of the nuclear triad in the next 30 years should be stopped cold, now, because he said, once you start, it becomes a dynamic of its own, because then you will have constituencies, with factories, who lobby their congressmen to go for it and so, I think that that is really very true. And I would really urge all of the participants of this meeting to help to mobilize against that.

Because the military-industrial complex, you know, it is a really a very important force. And Ramsey Clark has spoken on this issue, very, very meaning-

fully. And I think the only remedy to it is, we have to awaken the moral conscience of enough Americans to say there could be a solution! You can convert any factory, from producing tanks into producing some usable, useful thing, such as maglev trains, tracks, cabins, locomotives, tubes for these new maglev systems by which you can go in the future, in one hour from New York to London. I want to see these kinds of things. And the same with the auto industry: It would be very easy to transform it into other production.

Question: [follow-up] Yes, Walter Hickel, who was Secretary of Interior and Governor of Alaska, said "wars are just big projects." So rather than put your money into this big project, put it into *this* big project.

We Join the New Silk Road

Zepp-LaRouche: Yes, and I again can only ask you, please, get ahold of this pamphlet and circulate it as widely as possible, "The United States Joins the New Silk Road: A Hamiltonian Vision for an Economic Renaissance." Because the reason why I think there is hope that it can be done, is because of what China is doing—I know that if you only read the *Washington Post* and the *New York Times* you will not know what I'm talking about—but China has developed a new model of state, which is based on completely different principles. It's based on Confucianism to a very large extent.

If you read the book by President Xi Jinping titled *The Governance of China*, which is a publication of about 70 of his speeches, and other speeches he gave on his travels which are not in this book, there is no question, that what China is doing is producing a new model of society, no longer "Made in China," but "Created in China." They're right now investing in the rejuvenation of their nation on a daily basis; they're putting maximum emphasis on the excellence of the education of their students. They want to leapfrog technologies, to always be the vanguard in all areas. That's why they have the best Moon program of any nation right now.

And in a certain sense, they're not competitive. They're offering that model for a "win-win" cooperation to transform the planet. When President Obama went to Africa, he made a really silly speech: He attacked China, I think without mentioning it by name, but it was pretty clear. And the response of the Chinese media was to say that that was an infantile response; because why not join hands and together uplift this continent which is right now really in trouble?

There are so many common aims of mankind, so many things, like defending the planet against asteroids, finding out what is really happening with the sunspots. Maybe you want to talk about this a little bit more. Because you know, people should be scared of the real things. They should not be scared of irrational things, they should be scared of what happens to our small, blue planet, if we don't find out better how the universe works. And I would like to....

Wysmuller: That's why I ended my talk with the solar slide. The other thing, yes, put research where it counts. You have a real, potential threat you want to find out about.

The other thing is, take a step back, and decide for instance what NASA should be doing. Right? NASA right now is a shell of its former self. I think it's been hijacked by the climatologists, but that's a different story.

creative commons/© Guillermo Abramson

We should seriously consider a manned mission to Mars, landing a human being on its inner moon, Phobos; there are good reasons to choose Phobos. Here, a collage that presents Phobos in orbit around Mars.

Manned Mission to Mars

But what NASA could do, is resurge the technological drive that we had when we went to the Moon, and here I'm not talking about going back to the Moon, as much as I'm suggesting that we should seriously look at a Mars mission, sending a human being to the inner moon of Mars, which is Phobos, and there are some real good reasons to pick that particular moon, because it rotates around Mars three times per earth day, so that means we need less braking to land on it than we would if we would land on a planet. And when we want to come back, we would need less fuel to take off, because we're already getting a boost from the moon on its way around the other side of the planet, heading back to Earth.

That's the adventure part, OK? What are the real benefits? You look at what we did in the Apollo program, and the benefits that we accrued as a result of that—I think somebody at the Department of Commerce estimated that one out of every five jobs in this country alone, is dependent upon and utilizes a technology that we developed in the process of getting to the Moon.

People used to say, "We went to the Moon and we put $20 billion up there." We didn't! We spent that money on Earth. It stayed on Earth! It developed our technology; it developed medical sensing systems, imaging systems, communications systems, all these things that you now define today, as what humans

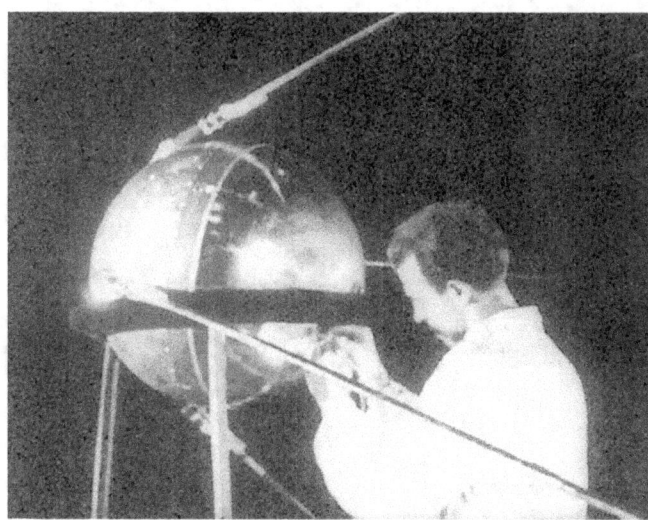

The Soviet Union electrified the world in 1957 by putting a satellite, Sputnik 1, in Earth orbit. "Sputnik challenged our high schools and universities to focus on science, engineering, mathematics. And our lunar landing was the culmination of that." Here, a Soviet scientist prepares Sputnik 1.

should be using and accomplishing.

You know, I can go into my pocket and pull out an iPhone: You think that would have existed without the space program? And the need for miniaturization and the movement away from vacuum tubes to transistors, to integrated circuits. All of that was a byproduct of one of mankind's greatest achievements. And the achievement wasn't getting on the Moon and coming back. It was developing the technology that *got us there*.

Question: I'm a little concerned, I think we need to talk a little more about what we can do realistically, and I believe there was a guy named Eisenhower who referred to the military-industrial-*congressional* complex. I could be wrong on that.

And I think right now, our biggest problem is the congressional portion. And I've decided to run for Congress at my advanced age and I would like to have as much support and get this material that we've been putting out here—I'd like to get that before the committees in Congress, and get some action to do these things. And I have to start here in this country; we can talk about grandiose things left and right, but that's not going to do us any good unless it gets through our Congress.

And I'd like to be, if possible, a point man to do that, but first I have to get elected. And I'm more than willing

to do it, if I'm elected, and I hope I can have some support from people like this organization and others.

Audience: Where are you running from?

Question: [follow-up] West Virginia's 2nd District. I am nothin' but a po' West Virginia hillbilly boy. Although some of my West Point classmates thought that being two reports away from Jack Welch at GE was worth four stars; but I said, "No guys, it's only three." (Got to have a little humor at some point.)

Vicious 'Carbon' Fraud

Wysmuller: Well, let me remind you that The Right Climate Stuff (TRCS) group has made its skillset available to *any* politician, *any* party, running for any office, who wants to get a good handle on what climate is really about. And I am more than happy to send you slides and things like that, that you can use in your campaign; I think, I hope you've learned a little bit of what climate is really about today; there's a lot more.

Question: [follow-up] I certainly have. I was walking through the halls of Congress, and a guy by the name of Steve Scalise announced that his biggest problem was reducing carbon emissions. And I'm not sure that that's true any more, after listening to this!

Wysmuller: Hang on. There's a difference. The carbon emissions include carcinogens, particulates, toxins, and other things that may have a carbon link to them. I was talking about CO_2, carbon dioxide. That's what you're exhaling right now; it's what makes plants grow. It has been conflated with carbon pollution, and that's the fraudulent part of it. They are basically mixing some real poisons that we ought to be concerned about, with things that make us healthy.

And it's the lack of science understanding that I think is a *big* problem in this country. It's what we overcame when Sputnik challenged the technical skills of our country. It challenged the high schools, and the universities to focus on science, engineering, mathematics. And our lunar landing was the culmination of that.

I think a Martian moon-landing at first, would be a beautiful way to reignite that kind of research, that kind of energy, make jobs that are *meaningful* for people, because there's a goal at the end. And the goal, like I say, is not just getting to Mars, but the development of the technology that would get you there.

So if you want that climate help, I will be *more* than pleased to talk to you. And I can find 30 other guys who'll do the same thing; and women, too, by the way. We have some very highly capable women engineers and scientists in the TRCS group.

Make sure you get my card before you leave.

Question: [follow-up] That's what I was about to say. I need one of your cards and you need some of mine.

The other thing, the nuclear war. We need to do a number of things, and I am surprised that the word about China that you're giving, is completely different from what the press is giving. I say that surprisingly. You realize that this country has educated 50,000 Chinese engineers in the best schools here. And I believe that they are probably not sitting in China playing Tiddly-winks. So we do have a real challenge ahead of us, and we do need to clearly reinvent the science/math curriculum, principally for our schools that we have lost in the interim.

People were mentioning Franklin D. Roosevelt. There are a number of policies that he implemented that would move us out of this incoming depression, and put people back to work. In my state that I'm going to hopefully represent, 41% of its workforce is no longer counted as "unemployed," because there is no—they're not on unemployment any more, and there are no jobs for them to look for. So that is not a good situation. And it's under-reported by the government and that's one of the major issues I'm going after.

And as far as nuclear things go, I have a little experience: I once was in charge of guarding a nuclear storage site in Europe. So this is real! And we need to minimize that. And I'm surprised that we're close to that again.

NASA Shut Down in 1972

Question: I must say that this latest discussion brought to my mind a very important point, and a thing that's been troubling me for *decades*, now. My first job when I went to work after graduating from City College in New York, was to work at the National Advisory Committee for Aeronautics (NACA), which became

U.S. Atomic Energy Commission

The government destroyed NASA in 1972, cutting its budget in half. In the process, it killed the nuclear propulsion rocket program. The Space Nuclear Propulsion Office had already certified the NERVA rocket engine for a human mission to Mars. Here, a mockup of a NERVA engine.

NASA in 1958. And I was working on the development of nuclear rocket propulsion, a joint office of NASA and the Atomic Energy Commission; I headed that office.

And we developed the nuclear rocket so that in 1969, I said, "Well! We're ready to start planning for missions to Mars!" Now, I go to various meetings in NASA and AEC and all of them, and I keep saying, "are we ever going to think about humans to Mars?" because that's the position I had taken at that time; we're ready to start planning for that.

Wysmuller: I salute you for that.

Question: [follow-up] And in 1972, they killed the nuclear rocket development program! I don't understand that at all. They're not really working on it. They're using nuclear propulsion in various small ways, the isotopes and various things like that. But they've killed the whole reactor development which we had proven out in Jackass Flats in Nevada. It was already there!

Wysmuller: Keep in mind, in 1972 they took the whole program out. They decided *not* to fly Apollo 18 which was ready to go; they had astronauts selected and everything. They sliced the NASA budget *in half.* We had 34,000 people in '71; we ended up with 14,000 three years later. And I was one of the victims, by the way, or casualties—whatever you want to call it, because that's when I left the agency. I didn't have sufficient seniority. It was the old NACA guys who were keeping me from staying at NASA. [laughter] That's OK, that's OK.

I ended up at Pratt & Whitney and had an interesting career after that.

But you're absolutely right: '72 was the key year. You hit the nail on the head.

Zepp-LaRouche: People have to realize that China has just concluded a sale of a commercial high-temperature reactor without having one operating; they had a research reactor which I happen to have seen when they did the excavation in '96 at the outskirts of Beijing, and now it's functioning, and they're selling it as an export item.

So China is going ahead, and if America doesn't want to fall back into the Stone Age, I think we have to turn this situation around.

So we will hopefully get all of you onboard to create a Renaissance movement, because that's what we need. I think we need a Renaissance movement in the United States. It's almost like the famous elephant and the

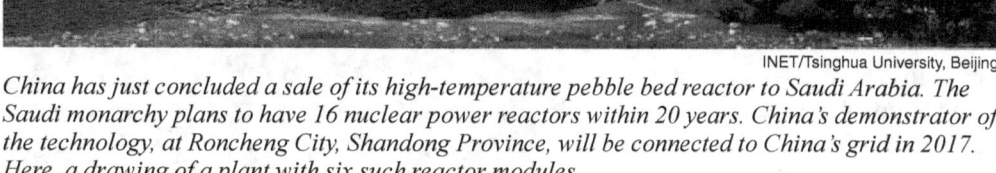

INET/Tsinghua University, Beijing

China has just concluded a sale of its high-temperature pebble bed reactor to Saudi Arabia. The Saudi monarchy plans to have 16 nuclear power reactors within 20 years. China's demonstrator of the technology, at Roncheng City, Shandong Province, will be connected to China's grid in 2017. Here, a drawing of a plant with six such reactor modules.

blind men; people are in their fields of specialty, and they see how this was dismantled, how that was destroyed.

It's the British Empire

But you have to look at the whole elephant, and the elephant is the British Empire. The reason they commit this swindle on the climate change, as we wrote that in our report, is genocide! Because if you decarbonize the world economy, which is what this guy Hans Joachim Schellnhuber is advertising, the population carrying capacity of the Earth will only be a billion people or less.

If you take all carbon fossil fuels—and they are also anti-nuclear, naturally—if you only go to alternative energies, you kill people! What is the refugee crisis, what is the failed wars, other than killing people? What are the drug epidemic? Why are people so stupid? It is really true! If you look at the entertainment industry, it is not to entertain people, it's designed to make people stupid!

Wysmuller: Yes, look at some of the video games they're selling kids, and you'll see them shooting, shooting, shooting, killing, killing, killing, killing. That's not the way a functioning society can function, can work.

Audience: That isn't something real!

Zepp-LaRouche: So that's why I'm really appealing to all of you: Join our choruses. You may think you are too old for this, or too young. We are creating a Renaissance movement in Manhattan; we are doing the same thing now in Berlin, in Paris, in other places where we can build Classical choruses.

Reaching the People With Classical Music

Billington: Our organization in New York and what we call the Manhattan Project—which is largely focussed on creating a cultural revolution and doing it through great Classical music—conducted a free concert in two leading churches—one in Brooklyn and one in Manhattan in late December—for which we have a DVD sitting out on the table there. I think they're $10 or something

I encourage you to watch this. It's not just a "good performance" of the *Messiah*. It's at Classical, Verdi tuning, not the high pitch that they've driven up since the time of Goebbels. This concert represented a reaching out into the population, pulling that population in through music to find in themselves that power of creativity which is driven out of them, day after day after day, by the ugliness of this culture.

And in doing so, believe me, we see it's working: This is creating a movement which is not just for New York, it's not just for America. It's global, it has the impact, not just amongst the people there, but all of those who are able to be part of it through watching it, through being part of our movement, to recognize what a real future would be if we create it, through the creativity in our minds, and not simply follow along in a pragmatic way of what seems possible.

So on your way out, add that to the list of things I encouraged you to pick up.

Question: [Lawrence Freeman] I have a question for each of the speakers. Helga talked about the propaganda against China and China's economy. One of the parts of that propaganda now is that quote "China's collapse" is now effecting a collapse in the economies throughout Africa. And so there have been dozens of articles in the last several weeks, including one in the *New York Times* today, blaming the "collapse of the

EIRNS/Stuart Lewis
With our choruses, we are creating a Renaissance movement in Manhattan, and also now in Berlin, Paris, and elsewhere, so that people can find in themselves "that power of creativity which is driven out of them, day after day after day, by the ugliness of this culture."

rising economies of Africa" on China. So I thought that maybe you could analyze and provide an answer to that particular narrative.

Blind to the Climate Hoax

Mr. Wysmuller, on climate change, I talk to a lot of people in the UN, in Washington, and in Africa, who are reasonably intelligent people. But on climate change, they become completely irrational and they have accepted every aspect of the propaganda. And otherwise, they can at least be encouraged to think on other issues, but on this, they've become so completely brainwashed and dogmatic,—you must have run into this. And I wonder if you might want to say something about how to deal with it?

Wysmuller: I run into it all the time. This arose from a conscious effort to seek revenue from companies that produce energy. How do you get the public to buy into that? What you do is you propagandize the average person, including school children. And if you notice, the syllabus that your children are learning from or learning from has been orchestrated and controlled, to all include this "climate education"! If you can get the public to come to you and say, "we need a tax to prevent this," it could be sea-level rise, it could be a lot of other things, the request to ask for a tax is wonderfully accepted by politicians as "Yes, we will give it to you!"

And all these countries have signed on, because they are all revenue hungry—every one of them. They're looking for additional revenue that the public does not mind giving them. So if they're willing to accept a gasoline tax that's a nickel higher or a dime higher, hey, that's all fine! I think that is one of the fringe benefits of lots of countries getting behind it.

The rest is, I think, more insidious. It is actually changing a culture in people that is *not* science-oriented. They're talking about putting windmills that produce one one-hundredth of the energy that you need at a utility scale, to power the world. Our President goes to Africa and makes a speech in Soweto, June 29, 2013; now, I'm paraphrasing it. I can't quite get it right, but to a group of African students he said something like "You guys don't need cars and air conditioners until we figure out a different way how to power them. Then maybe you'll get them." The *hubris* involved in that statement is astounding! The fact is, those African kids *do* deserve to get cars and air conditioners; and for us to withhold them is ludicrous!

Electrify Africa

You know, there are people in Africa who are running around, or sending their kids out into the local forest, gathering up firewood to boil the water, so their kids won't get river blindness. And that's how they're living! To deny them power when we could electrify Africa, at a *fraction* of what we are spending and wasting on climate research—that's the paradigm that has to change!

And it's not just Africa, it's South America, Indonesia—lots of places. Why? Because we can get kids and school them! And they can find cures for cancer and other things that we will never know if they have never been given the chance to develop their intelligence.

We need the intellect of humanity, available to solve the problems of humanity. And by keeping two-thirds of world on a subsistence economy, you will *never* achieve that goal!

Zepp-LaRouche: Briefly on this propaganda against China, it is really absurd, because the United States manipulates statistics in such a way that is unbe-

Green University

"There are people in Africa sending their kids into the local forest, gathering up firewood to boil the water, so their kids won't get river blindness. And that's how they're living! To deny them power, when we could electrify Africa at a fraction of what we are wasting on climate research—that's the paradigm that has to change!

lievable. All categories of production go down, but then they have a "confidence index" which goes way up, and then they put this out as the forecast. You know, there are fortunately some European economists who have seen through this fraud, and there are many newsletters now, saying: Forget it, if you look at all the investments in Africa and in Asia that China is involved in, in the second half of 2016 you will see that these things will transform every place where this is happening, because it's based on sound economics. It's based on high technology, on increase of productivity of the labor force, on education. So don't believe it, and I think it's just total propaganda.

I mean, the *New York Times*, the *Washington Post*,—the *Washington Post* is lying! They just had three articles on why Glass-Steagall could not have prevented the crash of 2008. Just by repeating and reprinting the same document, which they did on two Sundays, doesn't make it any more true. This is spin! This is spin-doctor medicine, trying to nudge the people into believing different axioms.

Go to the website of LaRouche PAC and look at the presentation by Jeff Steinberg on the British Empire drug policies going back to Aldous Huxley and various other people, and then compare what is happening to the United States today.

This is a long-term plan to lower the cognitive potential of the population, which is what empires do. The

Roman Empire invented the circus, the gladiators, they included the population in bestial decisions about whether a gladiator should die or live, and in that way you make people *bad*, you turn them into evil people, because then you can control them more easily.

Media Menticide

As for the entire media, I don't know. Maybe they are 20% journalists. All the rest is "public relations," (PR). They have a certain belief structure they want to convey, and they run campaigns like a PR firm using every piece of information to spin it in a certain sense, until they have nudged, like Cass Sunstein describes it in his horrible book [*Nudge*]: You have a group of people sitting on one side of the room, and then, by the end of the meeting, they're all sitting on the other side of the room, because you have nudged their beliefs to group-think, they now believe they should sit on the other side of the room. This is manipulation.

And the biggest task we have to accomplish is to get people thinking for themselves again, so that they should have an allergy against group-think. Group-think makes people stupid. You know, you have clubs and people believe only the belief structure of their club, and if you don't go along with the leading axioms of that club you get kicked out, so therefore you adjust your belief structure to what this group of people is thinking. And that's what the neighbors are saying, or your colleagues, or your peers. And the number of self-thinking people, of *truth* seeking people, of people who are trying to develop their own minds in such a way that they may not know everything, but they know how to find out how to think—and I don't mean Google.

People should start reading books, again, do research. If you want to investigate any subject, you have to read books, lots of them!

Wysmuller: Let me add a little bit to that: I'll give you one example, and that's a club that I'm fairly familiar with, that's the Sierra Club. The Sierra Club used to be composed of people who really were true environmentalists: They did not want the environment hurt by poisons, carcinogens, or water pollution or things like that! They have been methodically, I use the word *hijacked,* to now be anti-energy, anti-development, anti-carbon dioxide obviously, but this is a total change from what the group really originally was. Protecting forests and keeping them pollution free, are very laudable

aims. But again, they've been hijacked into a totally different direction. I don't recognize the Sierra Club any more when I read their publications. I'm trying to persuade them to go back to what they ought to be doing.

But you see that in different organizations all over the country—this process of hijacking. If you're involved in a group, make sure it doesn't happen in yours, that you keep your mind intact, and your purposes clear.

'Accidental Launch' Now Intended

Question: [Jeff Steinberg] Yes, I have a comment and then a question for both speakers.

Helga, right at the start of your presentation, you mentioned Perry and the danger of an accidental launch of nuclear missiles. I have just finished reading his memoir. What he describes as "accidental" or "unintentional" has now become completely intentional. [*My Journey at the Nuclear Brink*, by William J. Perry; see Steinberg's review in *EIR*, Jan. 29, 2016.

What he basically says, is that we must abandon this doctrine of launch on warning, because given the provocations against Russia, given all of the crises, the danger is that if there is even a perception of a launch by one side, then the amount of time in which a decision has to be made about whether to launch a war of total Armageddon is now reduced to a matter of seconds. And what I'm afraid of, is quite frankly, that these are not even human decisions any more, but that these are computer programmed decisions where, in effect, the outcome is completely predetermined.

I was happy to get a fuller explanation which Perry goes through in this recent book. It's really not accidental in the sense of somebody slipping and their elbow knocks on the nuclear button, or something like that. There is now, an opportunity to avoid the danger. And there have been calls by Perry, by Matlock, by General [James E.] Cartwright, to bring an immediate end to launch on warning, and to the extent that's not being done, that's now willful. So I think the danger is even greater, that there's an opportunity to at least de-escalate the danger, and the decision not to do it, is a conscious decision on the part of the White House, the President.

My question stems from that little quick back-and-forth between the gentleman from NACA and you, because I hadn't realized there had been this total decimation of NASA in 1972. And Helga talks about a paradigm shift being urgently needed today; what's clear from the scope of this discussion, is that there was a paradigm shift that was consciously enforced in that early period. NASA was taken down, the Club of Rome issued the *Limits to Growth* book, there was the Bucharest UN conference on population reduction—in other words, there was a conscious, top-down onslaught, to change the policy thinking and the policy paradigm. And one of the things I was struck by, is that, had Robert Kennedy not been assassinated, it's almost a certainty he would have been elected President. I highly doubt that he would have shut down the Apollo program and halved NASA, considering it was the hallmark of his brother's Presidency.

Armageddon Closer than in 1962

So I'd like comments on this paradigm shift issue, because I think we're living through, now, the dying moments of a bad paradigm that, one way or the other, is coming to an end. And it's both a great opportunity, but the danger is greater than ever, and I think that's the larger context in which all of these establishment figures tied to the nuclear program have all come out and said, the danger of nuclear Armageddon is greater now than it was at the time of the Cuban Missile Crisis.

Wysmuller: Let me address the NASA shift, the extent of which is stunning, if you think about it. These days, when we had a shuttle program, that's been terminated, too. And people like to blame Bush and the current administration, but I can blame both Bush and Obama. Obama in his first two years controlled both sides of Congress; they easily could have gotten NASA back on a funding track, but the answer was no, they were going to continue that taking down of the agency.

Now, what do we do? We pay the Russians $100 million each, *per astronaut* that we send to the International Space Station. Now, this is $100 million of your tax dollars, and they're going to supply and fund jobs in Russia. A typical shuttle launch, for about $200 million—and a little more if you count salaries and stuff—takes seven or eight people up there, plus cargo. It's an *astounding* shift!

I've heard people defend this, saying, well, this is the only way we could have gotten the Russian space program to survive, because they needed that money. That may have been true, but you know, cooperation is the way to go here and we shouldn't be sending those American jobs that used to be here, in shuttle support and others, they're gone! These people aren't working

in NASA any more. They left like I did; they work other places, if they have jobs, or they're still counted in the unemployed.

But what happened to NASA is real. I don't know,—this administration is not going to be able to solve it. Will a subsequent administration change things around? I don't know. I don't have a lot of confidence in it, because there's *lots* of other things going on in the economy, and I think Helga's probably better off to address those. But NASA is a shell of its former self.

British Oligarchs for Hunger, Backwardness

Zepp-LaRouche: I think this paradigm shift,—if you think back, Roosevelt wanted to end colonialism at the end of World War II. De Gaulle wanted to have the French people involved in a mission to develop the so-called "Third World"; Kennedy, obviously. So you had a certain direction which I would put under the category of "good government," where the aim was to improve the livelihood, the living standard of the people, to have a moral improvement: You know, the old idea that you are working so that future generations have a better life than you. That was always the yardstick of morality.

And then, in this period, you had—in the '60s—you had the UN Development Decades, the idea that eventually you would overcome underdevelopment of the Third World; you had Paul VI with his Encyclical *Populorum Progressio*, which was the idea that you would overcome poverty, that you would eliminate poverty! Because poverty is the biggest human rights violation there is. Because if people die of hunger—Jean Ziegler has written very important things about that—that people who die of hunger, it's the most horrible death you can have. Because all your bodily functions gradually stop, and it's agonizing.

So, there was a clear commitment to overcome underdevelopment in the Third World. And I remember very well, somewhere in the '60s, there was a conscious decision by the international British-dominated oligarchy, to eradicate that commitment. And we saw it: It was the Club of Rome, which put out the lies about the limits to growth. And Meadows and Forrester later admitted that they had programmed the assumptions of their computer program such that it would prove that there are limits to growth. And they admitted that they left out the most important aspect, namely that what is a resource is defined by the technology you have.

So it was a fraud. That's how the green movement was created. And I remember, they transformed the '68 movement, and made it a green movement. They used social engineering. And it was the genius of my sweet husband, that he recognized in the '60s that the rock-drug counterculture would destroy the cognitive potential of society. And he was the only one who said that, at that time. Everybody else said, "Oh these hippies, they're so sweet, flower power, isn't that nice?" But he said, "no, it is that culture which will completely destroy the cognitive potential of society."

And that's how *this* movement was founded, as a conscious counter, based on Classical music, based on science, on natural science, and beautiful conceptions in literature, which celebrate creativity.

This other culture makes people stupid! Rock music makes people stupid. Drugs—sex, I don't know … [laughter]

Wysmuller: Well, sex makes people.

Zepp-LaRouche: Yes, it has a useful function, but mixed with these other things it is—definitely …

So, I think that the paradigm was induced very consciously. We have published an enormous amount of materials about that, including the invention of the "population bomb." People used to think that population is an asset: That the more people you have, the more creativity, the more people can develop expertise. If you want to have a modern, industrial society you need to have a lot of people, because you need a lot of different branches of knowledge being pursued in depth, and if you have only Luxembourg, you will never become a… [laughter]; you look at [former prime minister of Luxembourg Jean-Claude] Juncker, you see what comes out of it!

People Are Wealth

But I think the idea of people being a parasite, that idea was induced! That the fewer people, the better, because they are all polluting the planet, this is a bestial conception! And a whole green movement—we watched how it came into being: It was the Club of Rome, *Limits to Growth. Die Zeit* had a series of articles discussing the so-called "scarcity of resources." And I was at the Bucharest UN population conference in '74, and at that time, people were not yet green! All the left groups were left, they were Marxists, they were something, but they were not green. The Communists used to be for technology—can you imagine that? It's no longer the case!

EIRNS

"LaRouche recognized in the 1960s that the rock-drug counterculture would destroy the cognitive potential of society. And he was the only one who said that at that time. Everybody else said, 'Oh, these hippies, theyre so, sweet, flower power, isn't that nice?'"

No, I think that the real paradigm shift was the combination of the green—and Lyn has always said what is green is already decaying, and people should remember that.

Wysmuller: But that's the hijacking I talked about, you know? You take an organization that is basically interested in making sure a forest doesn't die, and you hijack it by turning them green, which means anti-energy, anti-development, anti-lots of other things. And that's happened to a number of—that's happened to politicians, they've been hijacked. I think the world has to—we need to be sensitive to that.

So, do your best to keep your mind functioning, and make sure you do that for your children too.

Billington: So, on behalf of everybody, I want to thank Tom Wysmuller and Helga Zepp-LaRouche for an amazingly inspiring afternoon. [applause]

Lyndon LaRouche: 'We Have the Ability to Change the Character of Man's Destiny'

Feb. 1—*The following remarks are excerpted from the* Jan. 28, 2016 Fireside Chat *with Lyndon LaRouche and the* Jan. 30, 2016 Manhattan Town Meeting *with Lyndon LaRouche. In these two dialogues, Mr. LaRouche defines the crucial issue of the U.S. Space Program, and the role taken by LaRouche PAC leader Kesha Rogers. He presents his comments both as a means for breaking open the U.S. Presidential election, as well as a larger peace-winning strategy for creating a new future for the human race.*

First, from the Jan. 28 Fireside Chat:

Question: Yes, good evening Lyn. It's Alvin, here in New York. . . . And I'm taking note that you are intervening directly on this, and advising O'Malley, helping him as to how to deal with this situation immediately, and to "keep his focus" as you're putting it, on his policy directly. So we have but a few days to go; people are putting in long hours to get this done and organize more people. But there's a real sense of optimism in doing so. They're really happy. . . .

One of the things you talk about in your recent leaflets the "element of a tactical surprise," and I was wondering if you could help us think more clearly if that's actually what we're doing in this process? And what else should we be doing?

LaRouche: Well, first of all, let's straighten some things out, because there's some doubts and some confusion about exactly what we are accomplishing and what we are planning to accomplish.

Now first of all, the point is that we have the two ostensibly leading Democratic candidates for consideration, but the fact is that our conscience and our intelligence

Lyndon LaRouche in a recent Fireside Chat.

tells us that the two so-called leading candidates for the position are bums. That is, they should not be elected.

Now, I'm not pushing the O'Malley election campaign as such. What I'm simply doing, is stating that I believe—and I know that other people believe—that what we have to do, is to actually get a correction, to indicate that neither Hillary Clinton nor her rival, are fit to be President of the United States. It's simply that statement: It's a negative thing; we're saying that this is not acceptable. Hillary Clinton is not acceptable! She's a bum, in political terms. She's not an honest person; she does a lot of lying; her immediate rival is a question mark: he's not a man, he's a question mark.

And so, therefore, what we're doing is we're trying to say, "let's open the gates." We're not pushing the idea that we're pushing O'Malley as such; we think

O'Malley probably should be considered for the Presidency. But we're not pushing him as a candidate. What we're doing is we're opening the gates to say that we have two guys running now, for the Presidency on that ticket, and we say neither of them is fit to be in that position. So therefore, we say we're organizing people to step out and join those people who recognize that we have to replace these two characters. We have to dump them....

China launched its first round-trip mission to the Moon (unmanned) on Oct. 25, 2014. The launch rocket is the Long March-3C.

That's exactly the way to put it; we are now looking down to Texas and other areas, we are looking to—take one case: Remember what Obama did early on: He shut down the space program! He crashed the space program! Now the space program was actually the basis for the physical economic development and maintenance of the progress of the people of the United States. So Obama, by attacking the space program and trying to crush it, destroyed the rights of the American people.

Now we had a lot of people out there who voted for Obama. They would crowd up to vote for Obama. That was a *terrible* mistake. It was also an *evil* mistake! Obama never should have been elected.

Now, we've got a chance to dump him. And therefore, we've got to ask, who is qualified to be a part of the leadership of the United States government? Our opinion follows, logically, we have to really go back to the implications of the benefits which were inherent in the space program.

Now, China has a space program. It's going for the back side of the Moon; it's a very important program. There are other things like that in the world. So we're going to have to reorganize the system of Earth; we're going to have to make changes in the Earth. We're going to have to go back to the space program. The space program is the secret, and we're going to do the space program, and we're going to do all the other things that Obama tried to destroy: We're going to bring 'em back. And I think we should look at it that way.

Question: This is from a guy named C—, who is a retired construction worker. He says, "Mr. LaRouche, as I am sure you are aware, the President of Iran has been in Italy and France this week signing big agreements for trade between Iran and these nations. This has included buying 118 new aircraft from Airbus, oil agreements, automobile agreements, etc.

"My question is I think this is a ray of sunshine for the world. It's much better than all the wars and threats of more wars we have had recently. What is your take on this? Is this on the level or is something else going on behind the scenes?"

LaRouche: You have to take two views of this matter. First of all, there's a policy which should be our policy, "us," shall we say. And that means, that we would be developing a program of the type that would be a resumption of the legacy of Franklin Roosevelt.

Remember that the Republican Party actually began to crush Franklin Roosevelt's Administration, and there was a deterioration under the various interests, the FBI and so forth, which destroyed, corrosively destroyed the rights of the people of the United States, dividing them by classes and classifications, putting some people down, and putting some people who shouldn't have been promoted, up; that sort of thing. It comes back to a point where we have to actually go back to the standpoint of President Franklin Roosevelt, who was my hero in 1930s and beyond; and he remained a hero for me, up to the present day.

So we're going to have to rebuild all of this. That's the way you have to go at it. We can do it; we have, right now, if we go with the space program, the space program is a crucial thing. Remember, what happened with the space program: Obama shot down the space program; and Obama also destroyed most of the things which were worthwhile defending, under Obama himself. There were a lot of other scoundrels involved, but Obama has been practically the borrowed Satan of today's society.

He's sort of a little Satan, but a nasty little Satan, you know, who kills—they have meetings on Tuesdays, under his direction, and they will take innocent members of the United States, and assassinate them, on Tuesdays! And it was the most momentous assassination, cumulatively, of citizens of the United States, killed and murdered by Obama!

So therefore, the point is, today, we have to get rid of the Obama problem. We've got to end the assassinations of the innocent members of our own population, and others as well. So therefore, the time has come for us to think about not only inside the United States itself, we have to think about other parts of the planet and say, we're going to take action to bring about a reasonable form, not only in the United States, but throughout the planet.

China and Russia Are Exemplary

Now, what's going on right now? The greatest degree of success is coming from China, and also Russia, and some other nations associated with them. In great part, the future of mankind depends upon the role that China, Russia, and their associates represent. That development is what is necessary to give the people of the United States, its citizens, the mechanism by which we can change the policies from what's been going on recently to what they must become.

In other words, for example, let's take the number of people who are suicides, and the suicide rates in the United States among the population is *great*. So therefore, we have to rebuild the population so they don't kill each other or don't commit suicide, which is what's happening; or killing themselves by the disease of taking dangerous drugs. So we have to make these changes in that way, and for that purpose. And we are also going to have to go back, and restart the space program. Because the future of mankind depends on the space program, not only for the United States, but for the planet as a whole.

You know, we live in a system which is not just an Earth system. The Earth system is something which is inside the Solar System. It's inside the water system of the Galactic System, and beyond that. And so therefore, mankind is going to have to exert influence and control over the water systems, for example, of planet Earth and beyond that.

And so therefore, we have a challenge, to recognize these scientific facts, and we have to assemble ourselves to develop the skills which are necessary to realize the benefits that that program represents. So we need a new future for mankind. It's not in some kind of screwball new future, it's something which is implicitly already there. We just have to unleash it. And I think China and Russia are exemplary elements, partially, of these people today.

We have to think from that term. We have to think of mankind as in the Solar System, eventually. And we have to think in new ways; we have to think about the future of mankind in new ways, ways that we should have caught onto a long time ago. But, now we have to soon begin thinking of those new ways.

Question: This is R— from Brooklyn. I just wanted to comment on the Dump the Trump rally; I was there with Alvin and the other people, and I feel we did make some progress and we did get people consciously aware that Bernie and Clinton were not acceptable. And we got quite few of the Dump the Trump leaflets out, and people were taking them, and there was less resistance. It seemed to be fairly effective. I just feel you should know about this.

LaRouche: Yes. It's true. But, I think, what I'm seeing now, in terms of what I'm getting, you know, advance indications which I'm getting myself in this connection, there is a very, shall we say, a surprising, immediate impulse to support our new candidate, or our new prospective candidate. And this thing can go very fast.

One of the factors is, of course, the space program. You know, there are people in Texas, and other areas, because the space program was very much built in that area. And we find that the space program was shut down by Obama.

Now, what we need, if we're going to deal with some of the problems of the United States, for example, and other areas, we're going to have to really rebuild the space program. It can be done. It can be done by cooperation with China, which is going in that direction, and Russia has always had an interest in that direction. Other nations are going into that direction—not in that direction but *into it*. So all these things are at our disposal, in principle. We simply have to make our wishes more efficiently known.

That's your mission; that's my mission. We must think in a global way, of how we're going to reverse the degeneration imposed on people of the United States; the mass death at a high rate imposed on the people of the United States, throughout much of the United States! We're going to have to fight, to build up that kind of reconstruction, that we had in the time of Franklin Roosevelt.

And I'm all for it, and I'm ready to go! I'm one of the most ancient men on the planet right now, and I'm ready to go!

Question: Hi, this is T— from Lake Arrowhead. I've got a couple of questions. The first one: I listened to an interview with the former Finance Minister of Greece, Yanis Varoufakis. And remember, as of last July, there was the heroic struggle of the Greek people against the European central banking system, and what happened is, after over 60% of the Greek people voted to defy the central bank by a referendum, but then immediately, the very next day, I believe, the central banks closed the banks and the head of the party, Alexis Tsipras, caved in. And Yanis Varoufakis resigned, immediately.

And Varoufakis is now calling a conference; he said in this interview that Greece could not take on the trans-Atlantic financial empire all by itself, and there has to be a pan-European movement for Glass-Steagall. And he is calling a conference of European progressives, to all unite in solidarity against the central banks, the progressives from every European country. And he has invited them all to come to this conference that he's calling which is in less than two weeks; it's Feb. 9.

So I wrote him—I'm not the only one that's said this to him, I'm sure a hundred people have—but he not only needs a pan-European conference, but it should

"What China is doing is a miracle!" Shanghai street scene in 1930 (left). The maglev train (maximum speed: 268 mph) leaves the Shanghai Pudong International Airport, 2006.

include representatives of the FDR/New Deal movement from the United States. We must all unite together against this financial empire. And I'm wondering if it wouldn't be a good thing to send one of our representatives to that conference—maybe Helga, since she more or less specializes in Europe. I think that might be a very worthwhile use of our time.

So that's just a suggestion. What do you think?

LaRouche: Well, if we want to win, which I think is implicit in your argument, if we want to win, for the Greek people and for other people who are also afflicted similarly; look at all the people there who are from Northern Africa and so forth, who are *dying* by being drowned in the Mediterranean Sea, drowned! Killed! In other ways! So it's not just the Greeks. There is a larger population which is subjected to mass-killing. And the nations of Europe, by more or lesser amounts, the proper nations of Europe, have failed. Russia has not failed; Ukraine has failed, miserably. It's been a murder operation, not because of the Ukrainian people, but because of the Nazis! And because the Ukrainian organization is dominated by Nazis, that is, actual heirs of the legacy of Adolf Hitler; and that's a problem.

But the problem, of course, is that there is no effective organization in Europe now to secure any part of the proper European nation. None.

So therefore, our object has to be to look at the whole picture, and how we can solve this problem. We have people coming, crossing the Mediterranean Sea, the whole area, and they're dying; they're dying *en masse*. They're being killed *en masse*. Yes, the Greeks are being killed; but what's happening to the Greeks is something that's happening to other parts of that community. Africa, same thing.

So therefore, what we need is a more comprehensive view, of how we're going to do that. Well, we've got a chance there. For example, we have two areas. You have the trans-Atlantic area, and we have the Russia-China area. As to the Russia-China area, China is really a very powerful force right now. What has happened to Russia, Russia has undergone a reconstruction which is very impressive, and the problem is, we have to bring together those forces which are positive, as a united force throughout much of the planet. That can be done!

And put simply, that can be done. What China is doing, is a miracle! What Russia is doing, despite the damage that was done to Russia in earlier periods, is also moving in that direction.

So we have the option, if we decide to do so, to create a global process of economic recovery throughout the system. We can do that. So I think the point is, we have to—rather than looking at things from the negative side as things that have to be beaten down because they are negative things—we actually have the ability, if we organize properly, we have the ability *to change the character of man's destiny* in a positive way. And that's not just some part, it's the whole business.

And the space program, the reconstruction of the space program that Obama destroyed, is the key to working with China, with other parts of the world, to bring about a *rapid economic development*, which is needed so desperately, now.

What Makes a Real U.S. Citizen?

Question: We have another question which came in from the Internet. It's from a young gentleman named

—. He's kind of searching for words here, so I'm going to characterize it a bit, he says, "Mr. LaRouche, I am a 31 year old man who has come to realize he is ... a modern day serf." Then he cites various things from U.S. history and he's basically asking, where is the nail in the coffin for the original intent of the United States? He's trying "to piece together the real story" of our nation and he greatly appreciates our movement and our "quest for the truth."

So, he's asking you to say something about what the core is of what makes a real United States citizen, as opposed to what we have today?

LaRouche: I can give you an example. First of all there was a whole period, Franklin Roosevelt had a great achievement; when the Republican Party took over the control of Franklin Roosevelt's organization, then there was a degeneration in general. And the FBI was the institution which became most prominent, as a destructive force, to destroy the productive powers of labor, in all senses of the United States.... I was privileged to be brought into a key role of the Reagan Administration. It was an arrangement; it happened before Reagan was actually installed. But I was involved with another scientist, a major scientist; I was involved, and the two of us were the center for a space program of a very special kind. And we had got to the point, where one of my roles was in particular, at that point, to get Russia to make an agreement on the use of nuclear weapons; that is, to end the conflict of nuclear weapons usage between the United States and Russia. I did that. And other people backed that up.

President Reagan did very well, because he was building up his organization at that point. And at the point that I was involved in doing the supporting role, for his development of his organization.

This was what we did then, and it's what we can do again, maybe not the same way, not quite the same thing, but the idea, the principle of that exists. And that's the way to look at it.

We had a great chance. But then Reagan himself was subjected to an attempted assassination, from which he suffered for an extended period before he was able to get back to full force. And shortly after that, I was dumped into prison, too. So I've been through that kind of thing, I know this kind of thing; I've experienced it, I've seen it. I've seen it around the world. I've had fun all around the world, in things I've done in various parts of the world. So I'm fully aware of these things....

Will we be zombies, or inquirers and builders? Yes, we can change the character of man's destiny. Above, photographer Michael Bentley captured what he called "Zombies watching TV." Right, students at McKinley High School in Washington, D.C., study chemical reactions.

creative commons/Michael Bentley

National Cancer Institute

I've been out of prison for quite some time, and I'm probably one of the oldest surviving men still functioning today! But the issue is, what I've known and what I do know, will solve the kind of problem which is most urgently needed not only for the United States but for the population of the planet as a whole.

We're going into space. We're going into space more than what people would understand as "space." We're going to move great masses of water, floating out there, outside the passage of Earth. We're going to go into larger areas of the Solar System, and we're going to do that. We can and we shall do it. It's an extension of the space program; we'll do it. And what we have to do is say, "well, there's only one thing you can do, do that. Do that, and then all the good can become available to you."

From the Jan. 30 Manhattan Town Hall Meeting

Lyndon LaRouche: We're going through a crisis of the nation which has no precedent, so far. And we're going to have to deal with things we're not accustomed to, and we're going to have to adapt ourselves to it very quickly. So, let's get into it, because I'm sure that those things that I just indicated, will appear as factions and fractions on the discussion we're going to conduct today.

Question: Hi, good afternoon everybody. Lyndon LaRouche, thank you very much for giving me this opportunity. I spoke to you before. My name is M—T—, and I worked as a liaison engineer at the Grumman Aerospace Corp., between ground support equipment and the vehicle. And, I'm very interested to see that we're going to have another space program like we had with the Lunar Excursion Module (LEM).

At one time, Grumman was hoping to get the Space Shuttle, but apparently Rocketdyne had a little better proposal; and secondly, Nixon was President at that time, so Nixon, being from California, it went to California.

So, I would like to ask a question: are we going to have another space program, like we had with the LEM program at Grumman Aerospace Corp.?

LaRouche: That was a very convenient thing for you to say, because that's exactly what's on my mind. The point is that, remember Obama destroyed the space program. He was the one who purposely did it. And people became stupid because they didn't have a space program. We had an inspired people in the United States earlier, and also internationally, with the space program. *And Obama shut it down.* And, it shut down the minds of people; it shut down everything of optimism in life.

And we see the results that have happened to the people of the United States today. Look at the number of people who are committing suicide-directly or indirectly—they're going into suicide; and children, young people, are going *into* suicide, and that is exactly what affects the United States right now.

And, therefore, one of my leading issues is the space program: Why? We have a member of our organization (Kesha Rogers), whose feature [?] is Texas. And, she is an excellent person, a very skilled person. And, she's back on the picture. Because now we're bringing in the question of the space program, again. And the space program is the secret of the mechanism by which we could bring the United States, and other parts of the world, into a recovery.

Question: Hi Lyn, it's Alvin, here in New York, as you know. Over the past few days you've been talking about how we should be shaping the institution of the Presidency. That's how I'm understanding the work we are doing now, around knocking off the two useless potential Democratic candidates, and moving and thinking that it has to be done in those terms.

But what I'm thinking about over the past couple of days, is how to get rid of Obama, because there's no guarantee we make it to 2016. And two, I just read that Senator Murphy, a Democrat from Connecticut, spoke recently at the Council of Foreign Relations. While he put it in diplomatic terms, he very carefully laid out the involvement of the Saudi monarchy and the murderous campaign they're doing in Yemen....

So this has to do with the 28 pages. The heat, you keep pointing out, is building up, that the Saudis are running into problems. How significant are Senator Murphy's remarks, even though, Obama is never, unfortunately, mentioned by name? So is this movement continuing to grow? Is there anything we can believe in that? Or just in general, what do you say about what I've just laid out.

LaRouche: I would say we have to get rid of Obama, and I would say that one of the factors of the process, which will do that, is we have a member of our organization who played a leading role in her own earlier life, and we are now going to recreate the space

The Chinese plan to mine Helium-3 on the Moon, anticipates its use in nuclear fusion power plants. Here, the Chinese Yutu rover on the Moon's surface in December 2013.

program. Obama shut down the space program. Obama's shutting down the space program caused the most catastrophic effects on the population of the United States ever since that time. Now she was very active in terms of the space program, defending it, and she's still there. And she understands that program. So, my view is, we have people who do have those kinds of credentials, that they have devotion to causes, which are essential to the people of the United States in general. And that's what we are doing. She's going to get back into that thing.

Before the space program was shut down, she was very influentially active supporting it in that area. As a matter of fact, her achievement of recognition was largely a result of her role in dealing with the space program. And she was part of the center of concentration on the space program at that time. She was a member, a voter, a supporter of it. But she played a very important role, and she was promoted to a relatively high rank, as a candidate, as a result of this operation, the relationship she had to the space program.

Now, my concern is that we have to get the space program actually going. Why? For many reasons—many essential reasons—it's not just one reason. What we have to do in order to get rid of Obama; the way to deal with it, is to deal with the space program business.

And maybe we can get some other Texans to come back to their senses and do something about that. We are relying on her to do what she has been trained to do, to be a supporter of the promotion of the space program. And the space program is a crucial part of the global policy of the United States. And that's the way I'm looking at it.

Question: Hi. R— from Brooklyn. As I reported to you on Thursday night, we were doing a Dump the Trump campaign on Wednesday, and we also put heavy emphasis on restoring Glass-Steagall, as well as the need for a more extensive space program, and the New Silk Road program. I'd like to know if there are some more irons you would want to put in the fire.

LaRouche: Yes, sure. Let's take one. There are many particular instances for this case. There are many parts of this issue. All right, one of the things that's happening is in the space program. Now China has a space program, and this program was to build up a Moon policy, that is, to develop the Moon. And this is very active still, today, in China. It's crucial, not only in China, but is crucial internationally.

And, when you go into this area, and finally not only does the United States go into space, but it goes into space with a very specific purpose, which is to understand what the other side of the Moon is. Now that has never been done before, except for certain experimental attempts. But that program of the space program, which is the Moon policy, and which is planted already as the intention of China—if that goes to work, once the landing of people or equipment substitution for people gets done on the back side of the Moon, you're going to see the beginning of a real revolution in space. So let's do it!

Question: Good afternoon, Mr. LaRouche. New New York City hot spots, replacing our public telephones, that you can see from 34th Street to 14th Street on Third Avenue, are going up. And they are called LinkNYC, and although they are called "municipal," yet they are privatized, taking about $10,000 monthly, to allow advertising.

The question is, can LaRouche Democrats look into the privatization that makes us peasants, and the public assets that makes us patriots?

LaRouche: Well, I don't see any problem here. I'm all for it, the results. And I will do everything I can to get rid of the bums who stand in the way of progress.

See, the problem here is to understand mankind. And people talk about what human beings are, what they mean and so forth, a lot of it's a little jazz. It is not the real point. I mean, because mankind is not what most people think mankind is.

Mankind actually has to be a creative force which does what no other species can do, with the creative powers of the human individual. And the problem is that the creative powers of the human individual are being suppressed, and have been suppressed. And what we have to do is get our rights back again in that thing: the ability to take charge of progress. Like the Moon shot. We don't know what we're going to find on the Moon. We have some intimation as to what may come on the back side of the Moon, but we haven't actually looked at it. We know some of the things that happen from there. We know some of the relations, which happen between the two. But we've never seen it, at least not to my knowledge.

And therefore the point is that mankind, by achieving the goals of the space program, which include, crucially, the role of the back side of the Moon, opens up the gate for mankind to discover the fuller meaning of the Solar System. And that's the freedom of mankind.

Overcoming Fear

Question: Hi Lyn, this is — in Manhattan. It was actually suggested to me, but it makes sense, I think, to talk about how most of America, in a way—and I guess by extension, it's really the world—is living through a Shakespearean tragedy of the likes of *Hamlet* right now, where the question is, as we've posed, everybody's learned FDR: "the only thing we have to fear is fear itself...." If in fact we are able to understand the universe, understand humanity, understand history in the sense that we can overcome our fear of doing what needs to be done, that then solving the problems themselves is not all that daunting.

And one of the examples that was suggested to me was Joan of Arc, the idea that she was betrayed, that she was subjected to the greatest amount of physical pain, that she was betrayed and more than that the humanity of the citizens of France were betrayed. And yet the idea is that she was in no way tragic, but she was truly human, truly heroic.

Now, in terms of thinking about that, I also reflect

Dennis Speed: With the scientists, musicians, and teachers who are coming around us, we have the capability to build the kind of organization that you, I believe, want to see in Manhattan. But doing it definitely takes your way of thinking.

on the tragedy of *Hamlet*, wherein, at the beginning of Act V, Shakespeare shows us the graveyard scene, Hamlet picks up the various skulls; he talks about Alexander the Great, he talks about Julius Caesar, he talks about his friend Yorick when he was young and he comments, looking at the skulls, about all the great things they did in their lives, for all of the impact they had on society while they were alive, asking: Is this all they are now? Enough dirt to stop up a hole in the wall or a beer barrel. And I think Shakespeare's showing us that Hamlet has no conception of the true definition of humanity, which is the complex domain which is fulfilling a mission in terms of what lives on after you; what you accomplish through what you contribute to society that creates a better future while you are alive.

And so, it seems that maybe it would be ideal for you to comment on that, because it seems like right now there are, for all of the tragedy that we're experiencing and for all of the opportunities for disaster that we have in front of us, we also have even more opportunities for success if we can just get past this idea of thinking about our physical lives right now, and saying, "what is our mission as human beings, and what is our mission as humanity as a whole?" So I would appreciate it if you could comment on that.

Thank you, Lyn.

LaRouche: If you go back in history, and you had a great composer of science in 1377, and he actually created, almost out of himself, the greatest discovery in physical science that had ever existed to my knowledge during that period. Here he was, surrounded by people who were great pretenders, and he would just invent everything; he produced everything. And then he died in the course of time.

But what happened was that the legacy of Brunelleschi, his legacy was one of the most powerful forces in the creation of modern science. And therefore, you find that in the course of life there are people who are sometimes able to contribute more or less greatly, in discoveries of things. And what I'm talking about is the fact that most people who are practical, people who have deductive methods, who have mathematical methods in the ordinary sense, they usually are failures.

Brunelleschi was not such a failure. He was intrinsically creative. And then, in the course of life, he died. But those who followed him, including Nicholas of Cusa, who was one of the followers of this kind of work that he had done, opened the gates for a great triumph. But what happened at the beginning of a new century, evil came in. And what Shakespeare was involved in, was trying to fight against that evil. He understood that evil. And he was fighting against it. And what he did, and what followed from that, from other sources in the same thing, this was the basis on which, the progress of mankind was created by *some people*—by some people, when most of the people, were incapable of accomplishing anything very useful.

And therefore, we have to depend on developing people, young people, and other people, who are intrinsically creative, and who will see through the folly of popular opinion. And popular opinion is the greatest threat to the existence of humanity on that account.

Question: Hello, Mr. LaRouche, this is H— from New York, and we did have some fun this week making fun of Donald Trump, who could have about as much corruption as you could have in one person! And I was also thinking, in reference to the space program, about the corruption of Obama, in that he gave the space program money to this billionaire from the Amazon corporation, this fellow Bezos, and another billionaire formerly from PayPal, Mr. Elon Musk, from South Africa or something; and they got the space program and totally messed up. Then when they mess up nobody seemed to care.

Another thing: this week I got a reaction from a friend of mine in Guatemala. There's a certain article in the *Washington Post*, but this is about a certain situation in Venezuela, which is not exactly our idea of a good government; but on the other hand this *Washington Post* writer seemed to have such sadistic joy in the way Obama and other people are destroying Venezuela and destroying the government and creating chaos.

So I think what's more interesting than Venezuela, is the mentality of these people in the *Washington Post* to just get such joy in destruction. I don't know if you would comment on that.

LaRouche: I can only make one economic statement on this subject: What's happened is mankind has been reduced into folly. Folly is a nice term for that, it's a polite word. I won't use the other word, but you can imagine for yourself what that might be. And the problem is we have whole nations in which the dominant forces in nations, the dominant cultural trends in nations, are degenerate. Europe is full of degeneracy; France is degenerate. Italy has been driven into degeneracy. Spain is degenerate, Portugal is degenerate. Much of the whole region of Europe is degenerate.

Now, what's the point? The point is, what're we going to do about it? And the question is, who can we find who will actually take the action *needed*, to eliminate those follies which threaten humanity now? It means you have to commit yourself to devotion, to *changing* things to get the evil of the stupidity out of the system. And the problem is, most people are so afraid that they won't undertake that mission. They would like to enjoy the mission, but they don't have the guts to do it.

And that's my experience in life. A lot of things I've tried to do, but I find very few people in society, who are willing to fight the *guts* issue, which I am familiar with.

Question: Good afternoon, this is Jessica from Brooklyn. And a little bit in line with what H— just said,

K.E. Tsiolkovsky Museum, Kaluga, Russia
"To get mankind to grow up." Here, Russian rocket pioneer Konstantin Tsiolkovsky (1857-1935), who understood that Earth is "only the cradle of mankind."

I was thinking about the idea that you were proposing concerning this whole thing being part of the population issue, taking away the population, a genocidal program. And I think if we really see it in that light—a lot of us still don't see it that way—but the entire thing is to depopulate the entire world. And it shows itself up this week in Michigan; they had a situation where they're taking, or most of the water supply that, I think, used to be from the lake, now they're trying to get that water supply from the river, which is polluted. And this is something that they knew was going to happen, and then they act surprised that there's lead in the river, and people are starting to get sick!

So we see that there are various things going on that are already known about, but people go along with these programs and don't know exactly what's going on, or why they're doing it, or why would you switch it in the first place. So if we really understand that everything is connected to the genocidal policy, almost all the things that are going on, are to depopulate. So we have to get Glass-Steagall in there, in order to make it clear to people that there are these connections; that if we *don't* change the way these things are going, none of us will be alive, even before they blow us up, you know, in the nuclear thing. [laughter]

So, if you could comment on that?

LaRouche: OK, well, I understand exactly what you're saying, and I'm sympathetic on that question. But at the same time, I'm more devoted to fighting, knowing that you have to fight, fight to achieve things that are needed by humanity. And I've spent most of my life fighting against people on that basis, on issues. And the only thing I think I've really ever accomplished has been to recognize how stupid most of my fellow human being have been. And I try to cure them of that stupidity.

Speed: During the course of the first 20 minutes, I was thinking of the space program, and I realized that you were saying something which we can actually immediately act on. Because, as you remember, back in September, when we had the press conference over at

Albert Einstein, "the model of the child who grew up."

the United Nations, Tom Wysmuller was there, we started a whole fight. . . .

Now, then, we have the music program that you keep emphasizing in Manhattan. And I wanted to say something here, because while we had that discussion on Sunday, you referenced something—you didn't say it exactly, but I want to say it—John Sigerson and Diane Sare, the combination that we had with that, and the musicians that have come together around this, represents—because of the work that was done, specifically that you inspired around the *Music Manual*—the whole question of the issue of tuning, this was a position on behalf of truth, a scientific position on the question of beauty as well, but the point is, we have that as a core. We have a process. . . .

So, between the scientists who are beginning to come back into play, the musicians, and some teachers, it's clear that if there's a clarity about what you're talking about on the issue of the Presidency, Obama, and what we've got to do now, we actually have the capability to build the kind of organization that you, I believe, want to see in Manhattan. But doing it definitely takes your way of thinking. And I've experienced, now over six months, seven months continually, this process where there's a correction, correction, correction—and as that happens, things happen.

So I don't know if you want to comment *per se,* on what I just said, but I wanted to say that, and certainly ask you, given our assembly here today, and things we are all committed to, if you have anything either in comment on that, or a conclusion for us here, now.

LaRouche: All I can say is, that everything I do in this connection, everything I'm proud of doing, everything I think is worthwhile that I've done, is all based on that conception. And it's to try to contribute to mankind, to get mankind to *grow up*: that is, to realize what mankind can mean, what the future of mankind can mean.

And the only principle is there, you know, we all die. Everyone dies. So the question is, what can be the result.

Let me just explain something in this thing, because it is very special: Mankind is of a different nature than most people imagine mankind to be. You know, most people think of people growing up, getting born, growing up and so forth; well, that's a nice story, it's a nice fable, but there's something else going on. It's the development of the powers of mankind, of the human species, the powers of mankind, to create the future—by whom? By people who have not yet been born. And it's the development of little children who have almost no knowledge of anything, but somehow under certain conditions the children that we give birth to can impart, create the future beyond anything that mankind has accomplished hitherto. And that is the peculiarity, of mankind.

The true peculiarity is, that if you can generate in a child—who's born but who you never knew—but this child actually made a contribution to the future of mankind, *that* is the purpose of mankind; is to discover born children, who succeed even beyond their own parents' achievements, to create something new for humanity, through their self-development. And this is the real genius of mankind.

No animal can do that! No animal can do it. Only children, and not all of them, but at least a few them. And that's what mankind depends upon. That's the principle of mankind, that we have the future in our hands, from children who will outwit us, in terms of their achievement. Sooner or later, they'll come around to it, like Einstein. Einstein's a perfect example of this case. He was a creative person who died probably prematurely in a sense, from various considerations. But Einstein has been the model of the child who grew up. [applause]

Every Day Counts In Today's Showdown To Save Civilization

III. The Doomed Trans-Atlantic System

Italian Bank Deal Postpones Eurozone Financial Collapse—But for How Long?

by Claudio Celani

What were you doing on Tuesday, Jan. 26? Were you expecting the collapse of the entire Euro system that day? European bankers and the European Commission were. In order merely to put off that collapse to another, future, day, on Jan 26. they suddenly pushed through a violation of their own rules. They decided to allow the Italian government to "bail out" the bad debts of its banks,— contradicting their new rules which came into effect Jan. 1, which supposedly ruled out further "bailouts," and required banks to seize, or "bail in" the assets of bondholders, shareholders, and even depositors to make good their losses. As in Cyprus in 2013.

The Italian banking system was collapsing on Jan. 26. But Italy is not Greece or Portugal, or even Spain. A blowout of the Italian banking system would have brought down the whole Euro house of cards immediately. —ed.

Feb. 1—A last-minute deal struck between the European Commission (EC) and the Italian government avoided an early collapse of the Eurozone on Jan. 26. A simple trick was pulled to allow the Italian government to extend guarantees on bad bank loans, temporarily relieving speculative pressures which were crashing the entire Italian banking system. However, the cause of the crisis, the bankruptcy of the entire European and Wall Street banking system, was not addressed, and therefore

the threat of an implosion was only postponed. Meanwhile, Italian economist Paolo Savona is calling on Italy to present an ultimatum to the EU, and if necessary to leave it before Italian sovereignty is totally destroyed as Greek sovereignty was destroyed.

European banks are loaded with one trillion euros of bad loans, according to official (and unreliable) statistics. Italian banks alone account for 40% of that mountain. But this is only a potential trigger, not the real problem. On top of the bad loans, there is an incalculable mountain of financial derivatives in the hundreds to thousands of trillions. Deutsche Bank alone reported over 22 trillions in notional value of over-the-counter derivatives in 2014. There is the real dynamite.

The mudslide on global financial markets unleashed by the collapse of the commodity and oil bubbles, has produced a bloodbath of bank shares in Europe, in many cases halving their prices. The introduction of the new EU bail-in rules in 2016, which forbid a conventional government "bailout" unless preceded by a "bail-in" of shares, bonds and deposits, has unleashed an additional run on banks, aggravated by the usual vulture funds shorting their bets on those same banks.

The Italian banking system has been targeted as the weakest point for economic reasons. Initially, the introduction of the euro currency had raised the prices of Italy's exports while cheapening its imports. But the

creative commons/Vyacheslav Argenberg

Headquarters of the Italian bank, Monte dei Paschi di Siena, one of the southern European banks hit by the flight of deposits to Germany, Luxembourg, and Holland.

negative effects of the post-2008 depression were worsened by the austerity policy imposed on Italy by the EU, through the Monti government in 2011-2013.

Then Obama's sanctions against Russia further collapsed Italian export industries. As a result, Italy has lost one fourth of its manufacturing capacity, consumption has collapsed, and workers have lost their jobs. It is calculated that 800,000 families are unable to make payment on mortgage and personal loans.

This is a large part of the banks' non-performing loans, which are officially at 200 billion euros, plus another 160 billion at a critical point, on the verge of non-performemance. (Some sources say the real figures are much higher.)

The rest of the non-performing loans are owed by insolvent firms in construction and manufacturing. These losses cannot be kept off the balance sheet, unlike the financial losses which the investment banks can hide with derivatives or by trading schemes.

Italian banks, with one exception, did not need a government bailout in 2008, because they were less exposed to toxic trading than other European banks, but are now threatened with insolvency because of the collapse of loans tied to the productive economy. And now they cannot be bailed out because the European rules have changed.

Capital Flight

Now, within the EU system, only a bail-in procedure is allowed, with which the Italian government had experimented last December, when four minor banks were put through a special resolution scheme which involved bailing-in (seizing) subordinate bonds of bank customers. The backlash was so large, that such an action cannot be repeated in the future.

The fact is that many Italian depositors have put their money in bank bonds, without being informed that they were to be considered as "investments" and thus, subjected to the bail-in rule. It is calculated that at least 30 billion euros of subordinate bonds are in the hands of retail customers. When the four banks were bailed-in, it was discovered that thousands of depositors had been cheated by being convinced to buy such bonds, and many of them lost all their savings. One pensioner in Civitavecchia, Rome, committed suicide, and this case shocked the country.

Thus, the government cannot allow any bail-in in the future. Moreover, the fear of a bail-in has caused a real run on deposits. Data put together by financial analyst Mike Shedlock show that large-scale flight of capi-

World Economic Forum/swiss-image.ch/Moritz Hager

On Jan. 19, Eurogroup head Jeroen Dijsselbloem and European Central Bank board member Andreas Dombret called for downgrading sovereign bonds held by Eurozone banks. The European Union intends to crush the nations that stand behind that sovereign debt. Here, Jeroen Dijsselbloem.

tal (deposits) out of southern Europe, especially Italy, is flowing into banks in Germany, Luxembourg, and Holland. The new deposits are in turn put into the ECB, despite the -0.3% interest rate of the ECB for such deposits. This so-called flight capital in fact amounts to an organized, classic bank run, such as Franklin Delano Roosevelt faced when sworn in as President in 1933. Analyst Shedlock explains, under the headline "Europe Fears Bail-Ins," that what is driving the large and growing capital flight is "fear of bail-ins, confiscations, capital controls, and bank failures like [those] we have seen in Greece and Cyprus. Recent examples include Portugal and Italy."[1] Euro deposits parked at the ECB increased from 36.6 billion euros in January 2015, to 196 billion euros in December 2015.

Especially targeted by the capital flight are Italian banks Monte dei Paschi di Siena (MPS) and Cassa di Risparmio di Genova (Carige), which are seen as candidates for a bail-in. Since the beginning of 2016, the Siena bank has lost almost 30% of its stock value. According to an article in *Il Fatto,* depositors with more than 100,000 Euros have pulled one billion out of the

1. http://finance.townhall.com/columnists/mikeshed_lock/2016/01/12/europe-fears-bailins-capital-flight-intensifies-in-italy-france-spain-are-german-banks-safe-n2102864 Analyzing the ECB data on the "imbalances" thus created within the Euro death zone, known as Target2, Shedlock shows this is largely flight money of deposits from those who are first in line under the EU bail-in schemes. Shedlock presents a chart on the ECB Target2 imbalances: the minuses, first Spain—"worst since 2012;" Italy—"worst negative ever;" France—"worst negative since 2011;" and then some of the winners with positive numbers, Germany—"highest since 2012;" and Luxembourg—"highest ever."

News Tv2000/Standard YouTube license

World Economic Forum

Paolo Savona (left) is one of the Italian economists calling for a moratorium on the bail-in regime. Ignazio Visco (right), Governor of the Bank of Italy, took the unprecedented step on Jan. 30 of demanding a review of the bail-in rules.

bank since Jan. 1. The rate of withdrawal is 2 billions a month. Liquidity at MPS has gone down from 20 billion to probably 17 billion, the "target" level of one tenth of assets. A default is not far away.

Had the Italian government not reached an agreement with the EU Commission, allowing for a de facto government backstop on bad loans, reintroducing a "Too Big To Fail" principle, this dynamic would have rapidly evolved into a major banking crisis expanding into a sovereign debt crisis.

The agreement allows a government-owned institution, Cassa Depositi e Prestiti, to buy credit-default swaps for securitized bad loans, whose price will be set such that vulture funds will buy them. Ultimately, the Italian taxpayer will pay the bill. The deal is another measure aimed at protecting the markets and not the citizen, and is not going to work. Only a Glass-Steagall banking reform is going to work, but this means that the current EU system must be overthrown.

To Destroy Italy as a Nation

EU authorities have already signalled that their intention is the destruction of the sovereign nation of Italy, in the same way they have destroyed Greece. On Jan. 19 both Eurogroup head Jerome Dijsselbloem and ECB board member Andreas Dombret came out pushing for a downgrading of sovereign bonds held by Eurozone banks. This is the proposal contained in the draft paper submitted to the Bundestag by German Deputy Finance minister Jens Spahn in December, as a first step before pushing for it at the European level. If approved, such a proposal would force many southern banks, which have a high rate of investments in the sovereign bonds of their

countries, to pay higher interest rates and increase their reserve requirements. Outstanding in this respect is the situation of Italian banks, for which the EU seems intent on aggravating an existing crisis. It also reveals the intention to crush the nations that stand behind that sovereign debt.

The conflict between the Italian government and the EU authorities has just started. The Jan. 26 deal marks a temporary setback for the Commission, but the conflict is set to escalate. There is a growing outcry in Italy to suspend or review the infamous bail-in rules. Economists such as Luigi Zingales and Paolo Savona have publically asked for a moratorium on the bail-in regime. On Jan. 30, central banker Ignazio Visco took the unprecedented step of demanding a review of the bail-in rules in a speech in Turin, revealing that Italy's financial authorities had warned the EU commission that implementing a bail-in retroactively would cause a dangerous backlash. Visco pointed to a clause in the BRRD (Bank Resolution Directive), which allows for reviewing the rules. The Commission reacted with an arrogant statement, saying that "there is no plan to change the BRRD," and "It has been known for one and a half years that creditor bail-ins would protect taxpayers."

There is no solution within the current system. As Proesssor Savona says, the Italian government should "take pen and paper and write down, as [British Prime Minister] Cameron did, what the conditions are for us to remain in Europe, establishing the date for a referendum after the deadline set for an answer. Will there be speculative attacks? We will prepare in advance, finding new foreign policy alliances."

The Italian government must also change its mind on Glass-Steagall, and lift the blockade on a Parliamentary debate on the various draft bills on banking separation, filed by almost all political forces. Just in the Senate Banking Commission alone, there are six bills which have been stalled because the government has pushed other priorities, most of them useless or destructive. They must take steps now against the coming catastrophe, of which Jan. 26 was only a very mild foretaste.

The Drugging of Americans Is Deliberate

by Debra Hanania-Freeman

Jan. 25—Americans are dying off in record numbers, especially those in what should be the most productive years of their lives. The leading immediate causes are drug overdoses, effects of alcoholism, and more direct forms of suicide. Especially drug overdoses. But how many recognize that this is deliberate?

Meanwhile, the authorities who should have been paying attention, have been very slow to recognize the problem. But since Jan. 19, when the Centers for Disease Control and Prevention (CDC) released its report, "Drug Poisoning Mortality: United States, 2002-2014," official attention has finally, belatedly, focused on the nationwide drug epidemic. In fact, the alarm had been sounded three days earlier on Jan. 16, when the *New York Times* published an article titled, "Drug Overdoses Propel Rise in Mortality Rates of Young Whites."

The *Times* article reported that after having analyzed some 60 million death certificates collected by the CDC between 1990 and 2014, it found that overall death rates for Black Americans and most Hispanics first flatlined, then began to fall. The numbers contrasted sharply with a shocking increase in mortality among whites. Propelling that rise? Drug overdoses were found to be driving up the death rate for young white adults, ages 25-34, making them the first generation since the Vietnam War to experience higher death rates in early adulthood than the generation that preceded it, even exceeding the levels experienced during the AIDS epidemic more than twenty years ago.

The recent reports also showed that the rise in white mortality extended far beyond the 45-54 year old age group that was reported by Princeton economists Anne Case and Alexander Stewart in November 2015. The Princeton report showed a sharp increase in the death rate for middle-aged white Americans since 1998, an increase the researchers tied to drugs, alcohol, and suicide.

Although these reports startled policy makers and Washington politicians, state and local authorities have been on an emergency alert for many months, as the body counts pile up and the death rate among young adults and middle-aged Americans—from all walks of life, all socio-economic groupings, and all job categories—skyrockets out of control. A survey of local media in every part of the country reveals a growing sense of panic over the heroin epidemic that has infected every community at an accelerating rate since Obama took over the U.S. Presidency.

Figure 1

Age-adjusted Death Rate for Drug Poisoning by Race and Hispanic Origin, 2000-2014

All Ages, Both Sexes United States

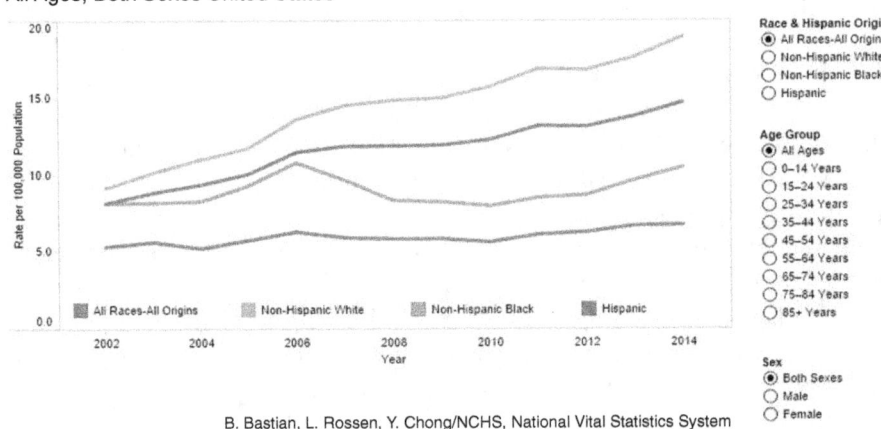

B. Bastian, L. Rossen, Y. Chong/NCHS, National Vital Statistics System

Heroin epidemic in the United States: In 2014, there were 47,055 deaths from drug overdoses. These data from the Centers for Disease Control tell part of the story.

Run from the Oval Office

New York State has released data showing the sky-rocketing of heroin deaths, from 923 statewide in 2003 to over 2,300 in 2014. Staten Island has the highest rate of heroin deaths of all of the five boroughs of New York City.

Ohio State Attorney General Mike DeWine convened an emergency statewide meeting last week, at which he warned that the state is now seeing three or four overdose deaths from heroin every week.

In New Hampshire, where the first presidential primary election will take place soon, voters say that the number one issue on their minds is the drug epidemic, trumping even unemployment and the overall economic collapse.

Both Wisconsin and Maine had already declared states of emergency due to drug overdoses in 2015.

However, none of these reports states the obvious. This opium war against the American people is being run directly out of the Oval Office, where President Obama has given the British Empire's Dope, Inc. a carte blanche to carry out a multi-faceted menticide and genocide against the American people. Obama's policy of non-prosecution of too-big-to-fail banks that launder the drug money for the Mexican, Colombian, and Afghan cartels is an obvious, impeachable crime, for it constitutes nothing less than complicity in mass murder (47,000 Americans died of drug overdoses in 2014 alone) on the part of the President of the United States. During the two terms of Obama's presidency, he has presided over a program of drug legalization, authored by one of his earliest political patrons, George Soros, a notorious British agent whose hedge funds operate offshore in the Dutch Antilles, beyond the reach of American law.

Over the last weeks, American statesman and economist Lyndon LaRouche has emphasized that what is occurring is the product of a cultural assault over more than a century against the population, dating back to the era of Lord Bertrand Russell, H.G. Wells, and the Huxley brothers, attacking the cognitive powers of the population—most recently through drugs, mass media brainwashing, and enhanced techniques like the killer point-and-shoot video games to which so many American youth are addicted. The result is a population that has been beaten down and demoralized to the point that younger Americans in particular have virtually no productive skills.

In a Jan. 25 editorial, the same *New York Times* that "sounded the alarm" on the current drug epidemic, offers its solution. Not surprisingly, it is *not* going after the banks that launder billions of dollars in illicit drug money. Instead, the editorial puts forward the same argument that the Soros drug legalization crowd has put forward for decades: that what is required is "a rational approach" to control the epidemic, providing treatment for addicts who want it and access to free, clean needles for those who don't.

What they do not—and for obvious reasons will not—address, is specifically how the drug epidemic aspect of this cultural war has been orchestrated. It is worth looking at.

When discussing the influx of drugs like cocaine and heroin into the United States, the names that come to mind are usually those associated with Colombian and Mexican drug cartels. Last week, the *Huffington Post* reported that Mexican drug cartels are flooding with heroin those areas of the United States where the documented rates of prescribing OxyContin and other doctor-prescribed opiates are the greatest. For decades, these cartels concentrated on trafficking the far more profitable cocaine. The American appetite for heroin was far more limited. So, what changed?

Meet the Sacklers and Purdue Pharma

As Jason Smith recently explained in "The Real Edition," in 1995, the year after receiving FDA approval, OxyContin accounted for $45 million in sales. By 2000, sales had increased to $1.4 billion. Not many companies can boast a product whose sales increased by 2,000% in five years! By 2010 OxyContin had taken control of 30% of the United States painkiller market, accounting for $3.1 billion in sales. The company that achieved these results is Purdue Pharma, the company which holds the patent on OxyContin and is owned and operated by the Sackler family. Indeed, it has made the Sacklers the sixteenth wealthiest family on a planet of 7.1 billion people.

The patriarch of the Sackler family, Arthur M. Sackler, was born in 1913. He graduated from the New York School of Medicine, simultaneously mastering psychiatric research and pharmaceutical marketing. By the 1940s, Sackler was using his background in psychiatric research to tinker with the minds of doctors, devoting his time and energy to finding new ways to get drugs into the hands of patients. He was one of the first to realize the marketing potential of medical journals, widely read by physicians, to influence prescribing patterns. Sackler also began experimenting with advertising on television and radio. This idea of the manufacturer persuading doctors to prescribe its drug was revolutionary at the time. Meanwhile, Sackler's two brothers, Raymond and Mortimer, purchased the small, fledgling Purdue Pharmaceutical Company.

At the time, Purdue made most of its profits by selling laxatives. Then along came Valium. Thanks to Arthur's efforts, Valium became the first drug to hit $100 million in profit. Finding new, off-label uses for the drug, Sackler was able to persuade doctors to prescribe Valium and Librium for purposes not approved in the original Food and Drug Administration (FDA) application. The profits were, indeed, very decent, but Purdue still wasn't an industry leader.

Arthur died in 1987, but he had taught his brothers well. They used their medical training to tweak oxycodone, a drug synthesized in Germany in 1917, to create a tablet with higher potency but designed for extended release. Using what they had learned from Arthur, the brothers set out to change the painkiller game. Eight years after Arthur's death, they submitted their application to the FDA for a new drug called OxyContin.

In the early 90s, however, there wasn't a lot of money to be made producing opioid painkillers since they were primarily used to treat cancer patients and those just out of surgery. Yes, opioids made a profit for the pharmaceutical industry, but in limited quantities due to a limited demand.

Manufacturing Demand for OxyContin

But brother Arthur's lesson was: "manufacture a demand." Establish not only a new system that gives doctors more freedom to prescribe narcotics for non-postoperative and non-malignant pain, but also an environment that actually demands it. Instead of fighting a losing battle against the existing medical framework, create an entirely new one—one that promotes opioid and opiate painkillers for everyday aches and pains—and work from within it.

First, one must understand the role of the Joint Commission on Accreditation of Healthcare Organizations (JCAHO), the most powerful accreditation institution in the world. Headquartered in a Chicago suburb, the Joint Commission is a nonprofit organization charged with setting the standards of care for hospitals in this country and accrediting more than 20,000 facilities in all but four states. It is tasked with inspecting hospitals—ensuring adequate care is being given and standards are being met. It also issues directives for care.

Lord Bertrand Russell, third earl Russell (1872-1970), the British Empire's reptile behind the drug plague.

In 2001, while the pharmaceutical lobby, led by the Sacklers, spent just under $100 million in lobbying efforts, the Joint Commission issued a new directive to its more than 20,000 hospitals across the country:

It is time to start treating pain.

And who did the Joint Commission bring in to teach hospital staffs how to treat pain? Purdue Pharma!

According to a U.S. General Accounting Office Response to Congressional Request in December 2003, the Joint Commission allowed Purdue Pharma to fund the "pain management educational courses" that taught the new standard of care for treating pain in JCAHO hospitals and facilities. And despite having been cited twice by the FDA for OxyContin advertisements in medical journals that violated the federal Food, Drug, and Cosmetic Act, Purdue was allowed to distribute materials to educate doctors on pain management.

With pain management now mandated by the Joint Commission, Purdue began funding groups such as the American Chronic Pain Association and the American Pain Society. These groups began demanding that doctors start taking pain management seriously, bringing their message everywhere from state legislatures to medical conferences.

Organizations funded by the pharmaceutical industry were created that rated doctors based on their willingness to treat pain and encouraged many family practitioners to begin prescribing outside of their normal scope of practice. The local family doctor suddenly felt pressure to prescribe powerful narcotics he or she might not have fully understood, or else risk a scathing review from a group like the American Pain Society that could irreparably harm his or her practice.

Rigging the System

To ensure legal protection for prescribers, pharmaceutical companies began lobbying state legislators who, with no medical background, began passing laws protecting doctors from malpractice claims for over-prescribing.

According to an investigation by John Fauber of *The Milwaukee Journal Sentinel,* published in 2012, the Federation of State Medical Boards (FSMB) accepted a $100,000 donation from Purdue for "printing and distribution" of pamphlets explaining safe use and prescribing of opioid medications.

At the same time that it accepted $100,000 from Purdue, the FSMB began calling for doctors to be punished for not adequately treating pain!

Purdue then proceeded to launch the most sophisticated and intricate pharmaceutical marketing campaign in history. Family practitioners were squeezed from every direction. The American Pain Society published rankings of doctors based on their willingness to prescribe narcotics, and the FSMB called for doctors to be punished for not adequately treating pain. Purdue had successfully turned the local doctor's office into a distribution hub for OxyContin.

Purdue claimed that OxyContin had less than a one percent chance of leading to addiction and didn't produce a high. OxyContin users, they assured doctors, were in no danger of building up a tolerance to the drug, a sure sign of physical addiction. All lies. And Purdue knew they were lies.

According to the GAO report to Congress, by 2003, primary care physicians—who had no business treating chronic pain—were writing more than half of all Oxy-Contin prescriptions. Pills were pouring into the streets. At the time, the Drug Enforcement Administration worried publicly that OxyContin was being prescribed overwhelmingly by doctors who were inadequately trained in pain management, but there was little the system could do. The system that should have stopped the problem had been compromised.

States across the nation, but particularly in the Kentucky-West Virginia-Appalachia region, were reporting wide-spread abuse of the drug. Addicts were crushing the tablets in order to snort, smoke, and inject it. Pharmacy robberies became common, with assailants by-passing the cash register and going straight for the bottles of OxyContin. Studies show that it was around 2001 when heroin in the United States began its upward trajectory, as addicts who abused OxyContin—many of whom got hooked unintentionally—found heroin to be much cheaper for the same high. Heroin or Oxy. Coke or Pepsi. Different packaging, same taste. Both will quench your thirst.

In 1997 there were 670,000 prescriptions for Oxy-Contin written in the United States. By 2001 and 2002, that number increased to 14 million, bringing Purdue a profit of $3 billion. OxyContin became the most widely prescribed narcotic painkiller in the United States. The Sackler family business and its sophisticated marketing plan, torn directly from the pages of the Arthur Sackler manual on how to influence physicians, was a success.

In 2007, the families of children who died from Oxy-Contin overdoses brought a federal suit against Purdue in the state of Virginia. At first, Purdue argued that they couldn't help it if people illegally abused OxyContin. But eventually, in the face of overwhelming evidence, they admitted that they had lied. They pleaded guilty to misleading patients, regulators, and doctors about Oxy-Contin's risk of addiction and its potential to be abused. Michael Friedman, Purdue's president, Paul Goldenheim, Purdue's medical director, and Howard Udell, Purdue's top lawyer, all pled guilty to criminal charges.

Over the objection of the parents of the dead children, Federal Judge James P. Jones, following the same pattern applied to "too big to fail" financial institutions that misled and robbed millions of Americans, accepted a plea bargain. Purdue was ordered to pay a fine of $600 million for deliberately misleading doctors between 1996 and 2001. None of the convicted executives was sentenced to a single day of incarceration.

The Sackler family, riding on a decade-and-a-half of OxyContin profits, now oversees a company that brings in $3.1 billion annually with a 30% market share. The family has a net worth of $14 billion. It makes the Forbes "Richest Families in America" list and we celebrate them. We name hospitals and medical schools after them.

The Sacklers and the Drug Cartels

But the Sacklers unleashed an opiate epidemic on the U.S. population and they did it on purpose. A 2012 *New England Journal of Medicine* (NEJM) study shows just how much the businesses of the Sacklers and the drug cartels such as El Chapo's Sinaloa Cartel depend upon one another. In the NEJM study, 76% of those seeking help for heroin addiction had begun by abusing pharmaceutical narcotics, primarily OxyContin. OxyContin, the report demonstrated, provided a gateway to heroin that had never existed before—a gateway that more Americans are passing through than ever before.

Purdue set them up for the Sinaloa Cartel to move in, and the American public never stood a chance. Yet Americans celebrate the one and vilify the other. The Sacklers and the George Soroses are called philanthropists. Barack Obama is still President. Isn't it time we ask ourselves why? A drug kingpin is a drug kingpin, isn't he?

creative commons/Smithsonian's Freer and Sackler Galleries

Centro Federal de Readaptación Social, México

A 2012 study in the New England Journal of Medicine *demonstrated that OxyContin use leads to heroin use. Here, the drug kingpins: Arthur M. Sackler (left), who masterminded the marketing of OxyContin on which his family holds the patent. Joaquín "El Chapo" Guzmán (above), the Mexican drug lord who led the Sinaloa Cartel.*

While the solution is not rounding up all Americans caught in the nightmare of drug addiction and despair, and throwing them in prison, neither is the answer to be found in management, treatment, and clean needles.

Any serious discussion about remedies has to begin with the fact that there has been a more than 100-year conscious cultural assault against the United States. The drug epidemic today represents the most advanced stage of that assault.

In 1995 both Mortimer and Raymond Sackler were named Knights of the British Empire by Queen Elizabeth II. Today, Arthur's daughter, Elizabeth Sackler, the current president of the Arthur Sackler Foundation, works directly with George Soros at the pro-drug legalization Drug Policy Alliance, and Mortimer's daughter, Ilene Sackler Lefcourt, is active with The Hastings Center for Bioethics, a leading organization pushing for the legalization of suicide and the "right to die."

When Obama was elected President of the United States, in 2008, with George Soros' money a prominent feature of that election, the message that radiated out to all the drug-producing countries of the world, amounted to an open invitation to start flooding the United States with even larger amounts of illegal drugs, because the effort to stop it would be minimal and eventually inconsequential. It's not just that people—out of despair, out of desperation—have turned to illegal drugs; those drugs were consciously foisted on them and are now available in vast quantities and at greatly reduced prices in every county in the United States. The 47,000 people who died of drug overdoses in the United States in 2014 alone, is just a statistical marker for what is actually going on.

Demanding Obama's removal from office for his complicity in this latest phase of this war against the American people is an obvious step. Restoring Glass-Steagall would eradicate the ability of financial institutions to profit from these murders. Once those steps are taken, our nation can begin to restore the Hamiltonian principles on which it was founded, allowing our people, especially our young people, to live lives based on the productive development not only of our economy, but of the very things that make us human—our minds and our culture.